"After his high school baseball career, Jon Peters experienced what many professional athletes have faced when their careers are over. He has a unique story of being in the spotlight—an eighteen-year-old, who broke a national pitching record and was featured on the cover of *Sports Illustrated*. This book is about what Jon experienced during that time and afterward, going through four arm surgeries and losing his dream. In this candid personal story, Jon shares his struggles and disappointments and his desire to help other athletes overcome their challenges."

—Nolan Ryan, former Major League Baseball pitcher, National Baseball Hall of Fame member, and author of *Throwing Heat: The Autobiography of Nolan Ryan*

"Jon's personal story is real, genuine, and powerful. He goes from reaching the top of the mountain to falling to the bottom, only to rise again. The way he shares himself is an act of true generosity. *When Life Grabs You by the Baseballs* is the story of a champion who never gave up on himself and created a life that is truly admirable."

—Bo Eason, former NFL standout, acclaimed Broadway playwright and performer, public speaker, and performance coach

"Jon Peters has written a raw and honest story about what it's like to be on top of the world, but to still feel empty inside. He reminds us that it's often in our brokenness where God meets us and offers us grace and redemption. You will find life, mercy, and hope as you read each page of his story."

—Melanie Shankle, *New York Times* bestselling author of *Nobody's Cuter Than You*

"Jon Peters says growing as a young pitcher was like being a snake. He got bigger and shed a skin every year. He got stronger, but on the inside he still had the same nature. This powerful story of soaring fame and the calamitous fall that followed ultimately winds its way to greater glory from the inside out. It is a path that all of us must find in our own way."

—Larry Dierker, former Major League Baseball pitcher, manager, broadcaster, and author of *This Ain't Brain Surgery*

"Insanely brave and courageous! This book is not just about baseball, this is about life. A selfless act to be vulnerable with the sole purpose of helping others is remarkable. A must read."

—Scott Nethery, former special assistant to the general manager of the Atlanta Braves

"How athletes are seen in the public eye is not necessarily who we really are. Jon Peters brings transparency to the intimate feelings and issues a lot of us struggle with."

—Woody Williams, former Major League Baseball pitcher with the Toronto Blue Jays, San Diego Padres, St. Louis Cardinals, and Houston Astros

"*When Life Grabs You by the Baseballs* chronicles the life of a genuine high school baseball prodigy who has an athletic mountaintop experience only to fall into the deepest valley life can bring. It then shows the hope that can be found when he realizes no mountaintop is enough or no valley can be escaped until we experience a life-changing relationship with Jesus Christ. It is a must read for any athlete, parent, coach, or fan."

—Lee Driggers, former head baseball coach at Brenham High School

"I had the honor of being a business coach and confidant to Jon for several years. After coaching athletes, celebrities, and influential people for two decades, it was quickly apparent that Jon's authenticity and passion, especially for kids and athletes, were like no other. So proud and supportive of his message in this book."

—Mike Lindstrom, J. D., speaker, business coach, and author of *What's Your Story: Discover the Man Behind Your Dad*

WHEN LIFE GRABS YOU BY THE BASEBALLS

WHEN LIFE GRABS YOU BY THE BASEBALLS

Finding Happiness in Life's Changeups

JON PETERS

WITH GINGER KOLBABA

Dedication

If you have ever felt like you were less than, worthless, lonely, fat, depressed, and/or full of shame and guilt, this book is for you. It's perfectly okay to feel what you are feeling. You are not alone. And you never have to feel that way again. I promise. And this book will prove it.

CONTENTS

FOREWORD

Jon Peters and I share a lot of similarities.

Like Jon, I became obsessed with playing baseball at a young age. From the time I was seven, I would grab a baseball and glove, head outside, and throw pitch after pitch against a brick wall. In my mind, with each throw I was pitching to the greatest batters in the major leagues—and I was striking them all out.

Someday, I told myself, *I'm going to play professional baseball.* That was my dream.

I worked hard, kept focused, and pursued that dream with everything I had. I had a killer slider—and I trusted in it to help me strike out batter after batter. For years, I lived that dream of playing baseball. Surgeries didn't stop me, other players didn't stop me; I was on goal and loving every minute of it.

But like everything else, my trusty slider ran its course. The career, the dream, even my own confidence eventually fell short.

Jon Peters knew the thrill of living a dream—and the pain of losing one. The trust he had in baseball—and in his case, his fast ball—only took him so far. When that let him down—as so many dreams eventually do—he came face to face with the truth of what life is really about.

Jon made some decisions that many people make when faced with the death of a dream—those decisions only brought more pain. Until one day, he cried out, "Uncle, God!"—"I give up!"—and he surrendered his life. And in that surrender, he found a dream and a life more fulfilling than he could have ever possibly imagined.

I understand the need for surrender. In 1995 I too found Someone to trust who would never let me down. Although pursuing and living my dream was wonderful, trusting and living for Jesus was far more important, meaningful, and fulfilling than putting on a uniform.

In the book you're holding, Jon gets real and vulnerable about being on top of the world and how great it felt to live a dream. Yet in the midst of it, he felt alone and insecure. He reveals the worst moments and the seeming hopelessness that accompanied him. But he also shares the healing, hope, and ultimate victory he discovered.

Of all Jon's record-breaking accomplishments, and of all mine as well, we can both say nothing beats putting our dreams into the hands of a God who creates dreams and whom we can trust completely.

Your dream may be to play in the major leagues and to have your name entered in the National Baseball Hall of Fame. Or it may not be. It may be to hike Mount Everest, start your own company, or be the best parent you can be. Your dream is unique to you.

Whether you're living it out right now and feel on top of your game, or perhaps you pursued it and lost it, this book is for you.

Whatever your dream is, one day you'll discover, just as Jon and I did, that trusting in that dream alone will let you down. You'll find that just when you think you can do life on your own, you'll fail. That's when God met me; that's when God met Jon. And that's when God will meet you too. In that moment will be the best time to look up and trust the God who created you and loves you unconditionally. The God of second chances. The ultimate Giver of dreams.

What is your dream? Where do you put your hope? Let Jon's story and the lessons he's learned encourage and motivate you as you pursue what brings you passion. And most of all, let his story remind you that neither dream successes—or failures—define you. That true happiness comes through trusting in and pursuing God's dreams for you.

—John Smoltz

CHAPTER 1
ON TOP OF THE WORLD?

"And pitching tonight with a record of fifty wins and no losses, number twenty-one—Jon Peters," the public address announcer shouted as he completed introducing the starting lineups.

I stepped onto the field and jogged slowly toward the center of the diamond as the crowd went crazy. Playing baseball in Brenham, Texas—arguably the baseball capital of the state—meant during games my ears were always filled with the shouts and thunderous applause from fans in the stands. Today, however, the noise was deafening.

I reached the mound and let the spikes of my shoes sink into the surface of the hard mixture of clay, sand, and dirt. I turned around to face the catcher. He seemed small against the sea of people, all in green and white—the Brenham High School Cubs' colors—to show their support. The regular stands were filled, of course. They always were. I was used to those crowds on game days.

But this was a throng; every space that could be filled with a chair and a warm body was. In anticipation of this record-breaking game, the city had set up extra chairs and bleachers, as well as extra makeshift concession stands, to accommodate the curiosity seekers. One fan even brought in a forklift, parked it behind the right-field fence, and added a raised plywood "floor" on which he set fold-up chairs for the more adventurous and trusting fans to view the game from an "upper deck."

People had even "saved" seats behind the home plate fence area. They'd snuck in hours beforehand with their folding lawn chairs and taped sheets of paper with their names on them.

I glanced toward the visiting team's first-base dugout off to my left. The roof was covered with media and heavy-duty cameras all pointing in my direction. Reporters from ESPN, NBC, CBS, and ABC hung out on the sidelines.

The coach had told us to expect more than 3,000 people at this game. I didn't care how many people were there, as long as one in particular was.

I looked again toward the bleachers to my right. And there she stood in the midst of the mass. *Jill*. The beautiful girl with the slender athletic body, olive complexion skin, and the bright blonde hair, accentuated by the two white bows set on either side of her head. The one who had been my girlfriend for the past three years. She was standing, clapping, and cheering me on with her wide, captivating smile I had fallen in love with.

I quickly glanced not far from her to find my parents in the middle bleachers behind home plate. Mom and Dad were on their feet, cheering. Even my brother had flown in especially to witness this game.

"You can do it, Jon!"

"Go, Jon, go!"

"Set the record straight, Jon!"

Like the sounds of popcorn exploding, I caught my name being tossed around from all over the grandstands.

All those fans, all the reporters, the hubbub and cheers. All of them—all of it—were there just for me.

Breathing in deeply, I took in the crowd, the noise, the scent of popcorn and hot dogs mixed with freshly-mowed grass. I felt queasy, as if I were going to throw up. But that, I knew, was normal pre-game jitters. After my first pitch, I would be totally in the zone.

Focus, Jon, I told myself. *You've done this a million times before. Don't think about all those people. Don't think about why they're here. Just focus on the game.*

We were playing A&M Consolidated High School. The Tigers had become a fierce district rival over the years. They were a good team, one we respected. One we were prepared at all costs to beat.

While my teammates and I were warming up on the field, we joked and commented that they looked as though they'd already been beaten. Perhaps it was the momentum of our team going into this game.

"They should have just stayed on the bus!" one teammate said and laughed.

"No way! We've got a record to break!" another teammate declared.

It was time to get laser-focused on the task at hand; I needed to set the record straight once and for all. No matter what had happened in the past, no matter what would happen in the future, I had to stay in this moment, keep my cool, and pitch the best game of my life.

The first batter stepped up to home plate, as the catcher, Craig Bolcerek, squatted into position, followed by the umpire who leaned in behind him. With a few practice swings, the batter took his stance and glared at me.

My arm felt good, strong. I looked at the ball nestled into my glove and then grabbed it with my right hand. The leather and the stitching on the ball felt comfortable in my grip, as though it were an extension of my body.

I glanced over at Coach Hathaway and remembered the words he'd said to me just moments before I headed to the mound: *"Tonight is an opportunity of a lifetime. Put whatever it is out of your mind and just go for it."* The simple reassurance that he was on my side and was rooting for me was exactly what I needed.

I was ready.

My eyes met the catcher's. His right hand dangled between his crouched legs and he signaled what pitch I was to throw.

Number 1—Fastball.

I nodded.

I rolled the ball around in my fingers, stepped back with my left foot just behind the center of the mound, pivoted my right foot in front of the pitching rubber, lifted my left knee toward my chest, took a stride with my left leg toward home plate, wound my arm back, and with my whole body's strength, threw a ball that sped upwards of eighty-five miles per hour toward my opponent.

Strike!

With two more strikes, the first batter was out. And after striking out two more batters, our team ran off the field in time to the chants and cheers of our fans.

One inning down, I thought, feeling pleased, but trying to appear cool and collected.

Inning after inning passed. With each strikeout, the crowd's frenzy seemed to grow. Being superstitious, though, as most ball players are, I hesitated to get too excited about winning this game, instead choosing to focus on one strikeout at a time.

Our team was good at offense as well, we could hit, so we easily drove in run after run with our bats. As the game progressed, the question became not who was going to win, but by how many runs.

Three to zero . . .

Five to zero . . .

Seven to zero . . .

This thrill ride had entertained the audience for years, with me as the pitcher, the main performer. I'd played many roles over time—a clown, a juggler, a trainer, and a magician. But on this night, I assumed the role of ringmaster, and it soon became apparent that the Tigers, who had been invited to this once-in-a-lifetime circus event, were being tamed by the Cubs.

I knew we were going to win this game. We had to. But a surprise seemed to be waiting for us. As our team's number of runs grew, A&M Consolidated's stayed the same: zero. Was it possible that this game would also be a no-hitter?

Now leading eight to zero, and moving into the bottom of the fifth inning, the excited tension hung thickly in the air.

Texas high school baseball had a ten-run rule that stated if either team leads the other by ten runs after five innings, the game is over. We wouldn't have to play to seven innings (the normal number for high school games).

The Tigers took their positions on the field, as our batting line-up got ready to take a swing at ending this game.

If the fat lady was not singing earlier in the night, as the saying goes, she was definitely humming and warming up her vocal cords in the background now. After a few hits and scoring a run, the scoreboard read nine to nothing with only one out. The game-ending run was at second base. My friend James, one of the best hitters on our team, and with whom I'd played baseball since we were eight years old, was at the plate. And how fitting it was that I stood at the on-deck circle with a front-row view of the potential final score. One hit was all we needed to score one game-ending run.

"End this thing right now!" I shouted as James stepped into his stance.

The crowd went wild with anticipation.

The pitch came at him, and with a solid swing, he missed. Strike one.

Another pitch. Another strike.

With a final swing and miss, James struck out. And I was up.

I didn't think the crowd could get any louder, but it seemed to echo off the bleachers and concession building and roar.

As I moved out of the on-deck circle with my bat, James crossed my path on his way back to the dugout. He smiled, not the least bit annoyed that he didn't win the game for us. "It's yours, Pete," he said, calling me by my nickname—*Pete*, short for Peters. "Go for it."

I stepped up to home plate. The game was now in my hands. I could end it with a hit and win the game. Or I could strike out and push us into another inning.

I didn't want to leave a man on base—especially when he was so close to making it home. Dietrich Burks stood just on the other side of second base, ready to zip to third and home as soon as I gave him the opportunity.

I took my time prepping and getting into my stance. I eyed the pitcher, blocking out all the racket and focusing on him and me and the baseball.

I knew the drill. He and the catcher were working out how to defeat me, how to get me to strike out. Back and forth they silently communicated until, finally, the pitcher agreed and wound up.

As his right hand released the pitch and the ball traveled straight into the strike zone, I swung with all my might.

I felt my bat connect to the ball before I heard its ear-splitting *smack!*

The ball quickly changed direction and whooshed between the first and second basemen and on its way into right field. I dropped the bat and took off running to first base. Before I made it, I turned my head back toward home plate to watch my teammate easily score.

Ten runs to zero. Game over.

My teammates charged toward me like a pack of wild dogs. Jumping and howling and grabbing at me for a hug. The media too rushed onto the field like a herd of bulls. The flash of cameras lit up the sky. I was pulled and prodded and yanked and hugged. So many people surrounded me, I felt smothered.

The crowd stood in amazement, clapping their hands, stomping their feet, and roaring.

It was the greatest moment of my life. I was now the United States' national record holder for the most consecutive wins by a high school pitcher: fifty-one wins and zero losses. In the coming days I would be on every major national news station. My photo would land on the cover of *Sports Illustrated*. I would be written about in *People* magazine, *The New York Times*, and even international publications. I would appear on *The Today Show* and *Good Morning America*. I was headed to play college ball and then on to the big leagues.

To the crowd and the media, to my friends and family, I had everything going for me. I was on top of the world and I had everything anybody would want: promising future, beautiful girlfriend, popularity, and growing fame. To them, I could write my own ticket in life.

What they didn't know was that less than twenty-four hours before, I'd swallowed an entire bottle of Tylenol, hoping to commit suicide. What they didn't know was that, although I hadn't succeeded at physically dying, I *was* dead inside.

CHAPTER 2
BORN TO PLAY BALL

My eyes sprang open at the sound of the birds singing. The morning light filtered through the wood shutters of my bedroom window. I hopped out of bed and threw on my clothes. No time to waste a good day like today. It was time to play catch! I grabbed my mitt and baseball and ran out of my room.

"Mom! Mom! You ready?" I found my mom sitting at the kitchen table, drinking her cup of coffee. She laughed. "Isn't it awfully early to get started already?"

"Na-uh," I said and shook my head. It was never too early to play ball.

She sighed good-naturedly and pulled herself out of her chair. "All right," she said, smiling.

That was all I needed to hear. I couldn't get my six-year-old body out of the house fast enough. I ran out the back door and headed to the place in our wide-open yard where we so often played.

I could hear the cows mooing as they grazed in the pasture surrounding our house. They were cheering me on, in cow language: *Go, Jon! Pitch your heart out today. Keep that ball moooving!*

I wouldn't let them down.

I took my place on my backyard "infield" and watched my mom settle into her catcher's stance. Loosely gripping the ball with the tips of my fingers on the tightly woven and raised red seams, I pondered what I was going to pitch. A fast ball. Definitely a fast ball.

The ball fit so comfortably in my right hand. As I squeezed it ever so slightly, it gave me a sense of power and strength. Twisting the ball to feel the seams with different grips and applying different pressures with my fingers, something my dad talked about a lot, I imagined the trajectory of the ball moving to the left, sinking to the right, and rising as it went straight.

I squared my shoulders, pulled back my golden arm, and let the ball go flying toward its target.

In my mind I could hear the crowds cheering as the announcer called the game: *"Strike-Out Peters is on the mound, eyeing the batter. He winds up, and ooh! Another strike out! This kid is the best pitcher we've ever seen in the whole, wide world! The history of baseball's got nothin' on this king of the mound."*

I nodded in agreement. I was glad the announcer appreciated my fast ball, amazing pitching ability, and my coolness under the pressure of the crowds and lights and fame. Oh yes, I was *it*.

With astounding precision—even for a kindergartener—I threw the ball at my mom's mitt over and over. And over and over. *And over and . . .*

I loved baseball. When I woke up in the mornings, my first thought was about baseball. When I went to bed, my last thought was about baseball. And all throughout each day, my thoughts were about baseball. It wasn't just that I loved the game; it was as if I'd been born to play it, as if this were my life's purpose.

After all, it seemed as if everything had aligned perfectly to make sure I fulfilled my destiny.

I was born in Brenham, a conservative, rural, central Texas town, with a population of eleven thousand people, located in the heart of bluebonnet country and halfway between Houston and Austin. Brenham was known for its famous Blue Bell Creameries, considered, unbiasedly, of course, "the best ice cream in the country." But more important, this small town was famous for its baseball and was often referred to as the "Baseball Capitol of Texas."

From one corner of town to the other, conversations among the locals never failed to include some talk of baseball. Between each bite of a hamburger and each sip of a cold drink at the few local cafes and watering holes in town, someone was saying something about the beloved game. In every crowd, at least one know-it-all, arm-chaired coach threw in his two cents, sounding as if he had invented the sport. Brenham loved its baseball. It was one of the only events in town. As some citizens would say, it was a way of life. It was all we knew. Baseball was in the water.

And I certainly drank my fill.

My brother, Ronnie, actually discovered the game before I did. Four years older than me, he and his friends would often start a ragtag game, to which I, the tag-along kid, who adored my big bro and wanted to be like him, would beg to be a part. Anything he did, I wanted to do.

My brother and his friends always seemed to have fun. They smiled a lot, laughed a lot, and were continually encouraging their teammates with chants, high-fives, and pats on the back.

Sometimes they'd let me join in.

"Hey, you want to play?" Ronnie or one of the boys would say.

I'd quickly agree. At that point, it wasn't so much about the game, but more a feeling of belonging. They wanted *me* to play with them.

Because I was so young, four or five years old, I couldn't quite keep up with them, so they let me be the umpire, or I'd shag—chase the balls. I was great at fetching foul balls. I didn't care what they wanted me to do, they *wanted* me. I was part of the team. I was somebody.

By the time I was six, something snapped into place, and all of a sudden I *could* keep up with them. For some reason I could throw the ball wherever I wanted. Catching was easy. Hitting was easy. And I fell in love with the game. I was good at it, people accepted me because of it, and I dove in completely.

On Saturdays my dad and I would watch the "Game of the Week" on television. I focused intently on the players' movements and techniques and listened to every word the commentators said. Between pitches and during commercial breaks, Dad and I talked about the game, from admiring a player's performance to discussing a particular play strategy. It was like I was in school and studying baseball without being aware of what I was actually doing.

Watching was fun but I yearned for much more than just being a spectator or an umpire or a shag. I wanted to be the main part of the show.

That's when I started hounding everyone I could find to play with me. For hours upon hours, my parents played with me. My mom, who was a physical education teacher at the local elementary school and a former college softball player, was my catcher. She was also my loudest cheerleader. "Come on, Jon," she would yell. "You can do this!" She was full of energy and never complained or acted like she wanted to do anything other than play ball with me.

My dad, who was a math teacher at the local junior college and a former high school track standout, assumed the role of my coach. He was laid-back, reserved, and quiet. But when he spoke, I listened; I knew his words were important.

As my mom squatted down, offered me a target, and caught pitch after pitch, my dad stood a few feet behind me periodically offering words of advice. "Focus on throwing to the target. Throw it right at the mitt," he would say.

And there I was in the backyard, reaching back and throwing as hard as I could. It was like I was playing a game of darts, hitting the bullseye smack dab in the middle with each pitch. More often than not, my mother did not have to move her mitt. The ball was right there. Precision pinpoint accuracy. No matter where she wanted me to throw the ball, I could land it exactly in that spot. Every time.

Our backyard was the perfect spot for a game. It was as though the land was created just for a baseball diamond to sit squarely there. Extending from the back patio of our house to the sturdy, four-studded wood fence that separated the yard from the pasture was the smooth, carpet-like, dark-green San Augustine grass. It was mowed a half inch shorter than recommended and resembled a playing surface of cushiony, artificial turf. The fence stood about four feet tall and outlined the yard's perimeter. It kept the Jersey and Angus cows my dad raised contained in the pasture. For my purposes, it served as the outfield fence.

Located at the northern portion of our home and adjacent to the covered area where my parents parked their cars was an unpolished, galvanized in-ground TV antenna. It extended into the air some forty to fifty feet high to receive signals from the local TV station. Other than not being painted bright yellow, it served as the perfect right-field foul pole.

On the opposite side was a large oak tree that stood in the pasture twenty to thirty feet beyond the fence. The trunk served as the left-field foul pole, often leaving it up to the imagination of the eye whether a ball was foul or fair.

Beyond the south end of our house and toward the pump house that contained the water softener, gardening tools, and miscellaneous equipment was a cluster of pin oak trees. They had joined at their lower trunks from years of growing in close proximity to one another. Because of their shallow protruding roots, a patch of grass in front was very thin, exposing a circular pattern of dirt. It was the ideal area for home plate.

In the middle of the yard was my pride and joy—a raised, circular area covered with a thin patch of grass. Elevated six to eight inches higher than the rest of the yard, the hump was the remnants of the collection of dirt removed and left over from the septic tank installation. Located smack dab in the middle of the yard, it served as the pitching mound.

And there it was—my perfectly laid-out field of dreams.

I couldn't get enough of the game. I was happiest when I had a baseball in my hand. Rain or shine—all the time. In my mind I was always the star, either striking out the best hitter to end a rally threat or hitting a long, towering home run to win the game. I was going to grow up to become the best baseball pitcher ever. If I could have slept on that field, I would have. It was the place, even at six years old, where I felt the safest, the most loved and accepted, the most complete.

But a game of catch only goes so far. I wanted to play *real* baseball—with a team. Not just be an extra hand whenever my brother and his friends got together. I wanted to be an essential team player.

"I want to play Little League," I told my parents one spring day, after I heard my brother talk about signing up.

"Sweetie, you can't. Not yet. You aren't old enough."

What? I couldn't believe what they were telling me. "What do you mean I'm not old enough?"

"You have to be eight."

Eight years old? But that's an eternity! I thought and inwardly groaned. I felt as if I were being punished and I hadn't done anything wrong. All I did was love the game with all my heart, was that so bad?

"That's not fair," I complained. I felt cast aside and rejected. I couldn't understand why they wouldn't make an exception. Did they not realize who I was going to become?

Maybe if I ask enough, they'll get tired of me asking and give in, I thought. It had worked with other requests. So for days in and days out, I'd ask my parents, "When can I play baseball on a team?"

No matter how many times I asked, though, the answer was always the same: "Not until you are eight years old."

But why can't I play now? I'd wonder. *Am I not good enough? Why doesn't anyone understand? Playing baseball is all I want to do!* "Please? Pretty please? Will you let me play?"

"When you're eight."

So while Ronnie signed up for Little League, I watched and waited. I figured if I had to wait another whole two years, in the meantime I would practice every minute I could.

If Mom wasn't able to play catch, Dad was always ready and willing. Or Ronnie would hang out and let me throw him some balls. I would play with anyone—if the cows or our dogs would have had hands that could have fit into gloves, I would have drafted them too.

On weekends sometimes my parents would take me to the Little League field, and I would pitch from the mound and pretend we were in a real game. When I was up to bat, my dad would pitch, but he would throw so slowly.

"Dad, throw it faster!"

He'd shake his head. "No, son, because the slower I throw it, the more you have to keep your eye on the ball." It drove me crazy, but it made me a better batter.

I played a lot of "cupball" too, which had the same rules as baseball, but instead of a baseball, the ball was made of paper cups that had come from the concession stands. During my brother's games I would go through the ten-gallon aluminum bins used as trash cans, recover the used, discarded drink cups, and smash them tightly to form a compact, wadded-up mass—a cupball. It usually took three to four cups to make a good cupball that would travel a long distance when hit or thrown. The bases were the trunks of trees or someone's hat or glove placed on the ground. My friends and I needed no bat, since we'd use our dominant hands to hit the ball.

When no one was available to play with me, no problem. I'd practice by myself. I'd throw tennis balls against the brick sides of our house, toss pop-ups and then catch them or hit them with my wood bat, or throw rocks from our gravel drive at targets—such as those cows (no wonder Sweetie the cow always chased me). With every throw, every toss, every swing, I pretended to be in a real game against real people, dreaming of the life of a professional baseball player.

Even just imagining it made my heart beat faster and chills of excitement run up and down my spine. *Someday I'm going to play pro ball and show everybody what I can do!* I'd think.

I was as good as, if not better than, the majority of the eight-year-old boys playing in the league, but regardless, I was not going to receive preferential treatment.

My disappointment slowly vanished as my love of the game grew with each passing day. Not being able to play on a team only caused me to want to play baseball more—before school, after school, and all day during the summers. I'd become addicted. Without baseball, I felt empty, lost, as if something were missing. But with baseball, I felt complete, satisfied.

"I want to play catch. Will you play with me when we get home?" I repeatedly asked my parents every day on our way home from school. On the weekends I would ask, "Can we go to the baseball field to throw?" They always found time to play with me, even if it was only for a short time.

Hearing yes got me excited as I would hurriedly find the gloves and baseballs we stored in the utility room. I was ready to play in no time, often way before they had changed their clothes or completed whatever they had to do first. I was their center of attention when playing and I liked that. One-on-one time with them made me feel wanted and loved.

Once we started playing, I never wanted it to end. But inevitably, my mom would rise from her catching position and announce, "Let's throw ten more pitches and then I have to go inside to cook dinner. We can play again tomorrow."

Ten more pitches meant at least twenty more to me as I pleaded, "Please, Mom? Can we just throw a few more? Please? This is so much fun." It always worked as we continued to throw more pitches before she finally put her foot down to call it a night and head off to her other duties.

As the "waiting period" progressed, I continued to pester my parents, my brother, and anyone else to play catch with me. I wasn't shy about it. *Everyone* knew what I wanted to do. I was always ready to play.

Determined to be involved in any way I could, I continued to shag balls during my brother's team practices, pick up bats during games, and even sometimes I acted like an umpire by calling "out" or "safe" at first base. Occasionally, my brother's coach would ask me to play during their practice if they needed additional players. Wherever he wanted me to play, I played.

Many times afterward, one of the parents who'd watched the practice would come up to me and say, "You're only six? That's amazing! You're so good."

I loved hearing that because I knew it meant I was holding my own, even though I was four years younger. Being included in their practices was an honor. I was bound and determined not to let anyone down, giving every ounce of energy I had.

Finally, two Septembers rolled around and I turned the magic number eight. Even though the Little League season was finished for that year, I could think of only one thing to celebrate for my birthday: I was old enough to officially join a team. That was great—but now I had more waiting. That fall and winter were the longest of my young life.

As spring slowly came, I obsessively checked for the announcement of the upcoming Little League registration. One Saturday afternoon in February, I retrieved the local community newspaper, *The Banner Press*, from our mailbox, ran into the house, and opened it wide, as I did every day. I caught my breath.

"Mom! Dad! Here it is!" I pushed the paper in front of my father, who was sitting at the kitchen table drinking his afternoon Budweiser while Mom was at the kitchen sink cleaning dishes.

My dad looked at me with a big smile and then he chuckled. He didn't have to say anything. I could tell from the sparkle in his eye that he already knew about it.

My mom continued her chores, and casually said, "Yes, we heard about it on the radio. . . . And *yes*, we will sign you up. It's a few Saturdays from today."

I ran with excitement down the hallway to my room, pumping my fists in the air. "I can't wait. I'm going to play baseball on a team. Yippee!"

The following weeks were nonstop chatter about my plans. "I hope I get a good team and coach. What is this going to be like? Will it be fun? Who all is going to sign up? What team will I be picked on? Will we be good? Who will be my coach? Do you think any scouts will be there? Will they let me pitch?"

My parents just smiled and nodded, probably looking forward to registration day as much as I was, just so I'd stop chattering about it.

I was up bright and early on that Saturday morning. Filled with anxious excitement, I couldn't sit still, instead pacing and watching the clock slowly tick off the seconds until 9 a.m., the time registration opened.

At 8:40, Dad walked into the kitchen, carrying my birth certificate to prove my age (the league was very serious about that age limit!) and his checkbook to pay the fees. He looked at me with kind and excited eyes. "Ready to go?"

Was he kidding? I was born ready!

I ran out to his truck, hopped in the passenger side, and waited for Dad and Ronnie, who at twelve was registering too, to catch up.

The fifteen-minute drive from our house to town was quiet, but electric. I could tell from Dad's constant smile that he was just as excited as I was. It had been a long two years of constant and relentless pestering to play ball. Now their time would be freed up because I would be on an official team with designated practice times. But it was more than that. I really felt as if they knew I was meant to play this game—and they wanted me to succeed.

As soon as he parked the truck on the side of the street, I hopped out and headed toward the building where I'd register. Dad fell behind because he wanted to double-check that he had everything we would need. Ronnie and I waited a few feet ahead on the sidewalk for him. Like a kid with ants in his pants, I bounced from one side to the other of the sidewalk while I waited a few seconds for him. He closed the door to the truck and walked to where we were standing. With a twinkle in his eyes, he put his arm around me and said, "Let's go?"

I looked up and nodded as we entered the building.

A line had already formed with kids and their parents who had gotten there before us. I looked around to see who was there. Surprisingly, I didn't know anyone. The kids were older than me. Silently, Dad, Ronnie, and I took our place at the end of the line.

As I studied the players I wondered whether any were my age. Would they be on my team? Were they as good as me? Were they *better*?

At 9 a.m. a lady with brownish-blonde hair and glasses and wearing a green Brenham baseball T-shirt and brown khaki shorts stepped into the room and slid behind the registration table to take her seat. Slowly the line moved forward. I breathed in and out with short, sharp breaths. Step . . . step . . . step—closer we inched to my dreams coming true. My hands were sweaty and my heart was racing.

Finally, we were next in line. I watched the kid in front of me talk to the woman as his dad filled out the paperwork and wrote a check. As they moved away, the woman behind the table looked at my dad and me. "Next, please."

I inhaled deeply as Dad, Ronnie, and I walked up to the table. Dad filled out some paperwork and handed my birth certificate to the woman. She looked it over in detail and then looked at me and smiled. "Are you excited about playing?"

Inside I shouted, *Yeeessss!* but aloud I could only manage a nervous stutter. "Ye-yes, ma-ma'am."

Dad handed over a check for the registration amount, which the woman took and placed with my brother's and my paperwork.

"You'll receive a call within the week from your coach," she informed us. "He'll tell you what team you'll be on, the practice times, and the schedule of games."

"Okay, thank you," Dad said. He looked down to me glued right by his side. "Are you ready to go?"

I nodded, and we headed back toward the truck, passed the waiting kids and their parents. And still I didn't recognize anyone.

On the way home, something kept bothering me. "Dad?"
"Yeah?"
"That didn't take that long. That's all we have to do?"
"That's it," he said.

The registration process was painless and fast compared to the years waiting to turn eight. I gazed out the passenger side window as the scene sped by in a blur.

I'm going to play ball. I'm really and finally going to show everyone what I can do. I'm going to be somebody.

CHAPTER 3
MY BASEBALL CAREER BEGINS

I was a Yankee.

The lady at the Little League registration told us we'd hear within the week and sure enough, we did. My dad took the call. "Yankee, huh? Jon will like that." My ears perked up immediately. This was it!

"Well, Jon," he said after he hung up. "Mr. Boeker is going to be your coach. Practice starts in two weeks." I breathed a sigh of relief. Alfred Boeker, now Coach Boeker to me, and his family lived across the pasture from us. I played sometimes with his stepson Ryan Bosse, who was a year older than me.

A Yankee. I finally had a team and a coach—in my mind, first stop Pee Wee Little League, next stop the Big Leagues.

The next day at school I found out everyone else had received a call too. And everyone was just as excited as I was. We exchanged coach and team information—there were ten teams in the league—mostly to start talking smack. "You're on the Indians? That team hasn't won since Texas became a state!" and "Yeah, I'm a Yankee. And we're going to take you down!"

I found out a couple of my classmates were on my team, which made me feel even more excited. I'd already played cupball and pickup ball games with them, so we knew how each other played. I couldn't wait for that first practice to come, and with each day I found myself filled with a growing mixture of excitement (I was going to play real baseball on a real team!) and anxiety (I was going to play real baseball on a real team—what if I wasn't good enough?).

Finally the day arrived and Dad drove me to Pflughaupt Field, the designated Pee Wee Little League field where our team would practice and play games. In Brenham, even Pee Wee Little League was a big deal—and it showed in the condition of the field. A chain-link fence housed a large diamond and a lush green outfield, and behind the home plate area, there were three sections of aluminum bleachers of about eight rows each. One directly behind, one on the left, and one on the right.

As we pulled up to the field, I saw the other kids with their dads hanging out and wondered how I would stack up against these other players. Even though I recognized and knew most of them—we lived in a small town, after all—I still felt anxious again. Playing cupball and pickup games with my buddies were worlds different from playing *real* ball.

Dad parked his pickup truck by the other vehicles. I grabbed my glove and bat and hopped out of the passenger side. We walked to the area behind the first base dugout where the others were standing. Dad knew some of the parents and greeted them. As they talked, and with the kids standing close to their parents, I couldn't help but notice I was a lot bigger than all the other boys. Bigger by at least a head. And wider too.

I found myself crossing my arms over my body, hoping no one would notice my size. *Why couldn't I be like the other boys?* I thought, seeing how athletic and little they all were.

I pushed that thought quickly from my mind as a tall, lanky, serious-looking man wearing a maroon and white cap with a "Y" monogrammed in the center, walked onto the field, toting a large camouflaged bag with a strap over his shoulder. I recognized him immediately. Behind him walked his stepson, Ryan, along with another man, Roland Wittner, and his son, Ronnie. My family was good friends with the Wittners. Once he reached the first base dugout, Coach Boeker dropped the bag. It clunked and clanked with the equipment inside it.

Looking at us, he said loudly, "Yankee players gather around over here. We're about to get started."

My teammates and I took our bags and jugs of water, walked inside the field, and placed our stuff inside the dugout, while the parents walked to the bleachers and settled in to watch our first practice. We circled around Coach Boeker outside the dugout.

"I'm Alfred Boeker," he said. "I'm going to be your coach this season. This—" he pointed to his immediate right toward Roland Wittner, "is Coach Wittner. He's going to be your assistant coach." Coach explained that he expected us to give our best efforts at all times and that we weren't just here to practice and have fun, but to *win*. We would practice twice a week and we had nine games scheduled for the season, starting in just two weeks. "We have a lot of work to do to get ready. So let's get started by taking a lap around the field for warm up."

Even though I was bigger and not as fast as the others, I wanted Coach to see that I was just as good, so I ran as quickly and hard as ever.

After the lap, we did stretching exercises—jumping jacks, touching our toes, pulling our legs up behind us, circling our arms, pulling our arms across our bodies.

"Okay, boys," Coach said. "Let's pick a partner and play some catch." Coach Wittner dumped the large bag onto the ground and out came batting helmets, bats, catcher's gear, and baseballs. I picked Ronnie to be my partner. We were good friends, and even though he was a year older than me, he and I had played together many times throwing and hitting. And he loved catching. He had the catcher's stance down, and when I threw to him, he knew instinctively exactly what I was going to do. We made a great partnership.

We threw for about fifteen minutes, all the while Coach Boeker and Coach Wittner watched and talked to each other. Every now and then, I'd sneak a peek at them to see if they were watching. I loved it when they looked over at me; I was eager to show my stuff and do well for them. And occasionally they offered a tip: "Get your elbow higher" or "Step straight to your target."

After we warmed up our arms, the coaches walked over to first base and called all of us together. "Good job, boys," Coach Boeker said. "I'm impressed with how well you all throw and catch. I think we're going to have a good team this season. Now let's take some groundballs and pop-ups. When I call your name, I want you to go to the position I tell you." He looked down at his clipboard and started naming names. "Ryan, you'll play first base. . . ."

I looked at Ryan who simply nodded at his dad, as though he already knew he'd have that position. He was left handed and a good athlete. He'd do well at first base.

"Ronnie, catcher." That was a given.

As Coach bellowed out the names and positions, I could only think, *Pitcher, pitcher, let me be a pitcher.*

"Peters!" he finally yelled out. "Alternate between shortstop and third base."

My heart sank. *Shortstop? Third base? Really?*

"And you're also going to be one of our pitchers," he continued.

I glanced over at Dad, who gave me a slight nod and a wink, as if he knew everything I'd just been feeling. Then he gave me a slight fist pump—a sign of his excitement and approval.

Pitcher! I thought and exhaled with relief. I knew our team was going to be good. Plus I was having fun! Life was great.

I sprinted to shortstop, patting the inside of my glove with my right hand. *I'll play anywhere Coach wants me to play as long as I can be pitcher!*

For the next thirty minutes, Coach Boeker and Coach Wittner hit us groundballs and flyballs. Coach Boeker worked with the infielders while Coach Wittner worked with the outfielders.

"Come on, Peters," Coach Boeker said sternly. "Let's go. Keep your body in front of the ball. You can't be scared."

Apparently, he didn't realize or care that we were only a bunch of eight- and nine-year-olds. He didn't play around or have any pity. He hit the groundballs harder and faster than any ball I had ever fielded. I wanted to impress him so I positioned myself again, determined to keep my body in front of the ball, even if it meant getting hit in the chest. I tried not to be intimidated, although that was difficult to do, since Coach was a hardnosed, intimidating, no-nonsense, kind of guy. When one of the balls accidentally hit one of the other kids in the arm, the kid was left with an indentation of the ball seams on his arm and an admonition not to miss the next time. I wasn't about to let that happen to me!

Finally it was time for batting practice.

"When I call your name, I want you to come in and get a bat and batting helmet," Coach Boeker instructed. "I'll throw you some pitches. If you aren't hitting, I want you to stay in your position and field the balls that are hit."

With each batter, he'd give a piece of advice: "Keep your weight back"; "Swing through the ball"; "Stop pulling your head"; "Don't drop your back shoulder."

When I was up to bat, I was ready to impress him! I was used to my dad lobbing the pitches slowly, so when Coach threw the ball fast, I either missed it or fouled it off. It seemed as though his pitching arm was about to touch me when he released the ball, it was so long. I'd never experienced such speed.

I thought about my dad's words, *Keep your eyes on the ball. Watch it closely all the way in.* And as Coach pitched again, I stared down that ball, swung with all my might, and *crack!* I felt the impact of my bat meeting that ball. All the way up my arms and to my shoulders little electric tingles swiftly jabbed me. And the ball flew into the outfield.

"Good job!" Coach Boeker said. "Next batter."

After all the kids hit, Coach called us to the first base dugout. He handed out the league-issued hats and shirts. "Good first practice! You all did really well. I'm proud of you and I'm looking forward to the season," Coach said with a big smile. "Next practice we're going to play a game among ourselves where some of you are going to be pitching."

As my dad and I drove away from the field that night, I thought, *One practice down and many to go! I want to play baseball forever!*

By the next practice, I was excited and ready to go. I'd always pitched to my mom and dad. But now I'd get to show my stuff and see how good I was against other players.

Coach gathered us all around, talked with us about our strategy and what we needed to work on that day, and then we started practice. We ran around the field and did our warm-up exercises. After warming our arms up, Coach set us up like we were playing a regular game.

I hoped our first practice game would find me on the pitcher's mound, but Coach placed me as the shortstop and put our more "experienced" pitcher on the mound, since he was nine years old and already had a year under his belt. I was actually okay with that, because I knew once I *did* get on the mound, Coach would be impressed. I just had to wait a little longer.

Even though I wasn't pitching, I was still having fun. I might have been bigger than the other boys and not as fast as some of them, but I had good instincts. I could always guess where the ball was going to go, so I was always ready for it.

Finally, Coach Boeker barked out my name. "Peters! Get on the mound. You're up."

I could have passed out from the excitement, but I did my best to act calm.

As I walked toward the mound, clinching the baseball and feeling the weight of it beneath my fingers, I glanced over at Ronnie. He smiled at me. With him as my catcher, we were going to be unstoppable!

When our first official game came, we were more than ready. Once again, Coach put me as shortstop and let the older pitcher play. Even though I wasn't pitching, I knew we were still going to win the game. And win we did. What a dream coming true!

Finally on May 18, our second game into the season, Coach Boeker announced that I'd be the starting pitcher. *Yes!* It was my time to shine, and with Ronnie as my catcher, we won 6-1!

Coach Boeker might have been tough, but that only meant more to me when he nodded his approval at my pitching or batting skills. And his hard work ethic paid off. We won almost all our games that year, ending the regular season 7-1-1—seven wins, one loss, and one tie. And I was 5-1—five wins and one loss. We went on to win the end of the season tournament too, in which I pitched every game and struck out more than a dozen batters every time.

With each game I pitched, it really began to sink in: I was dominating on the mound. Not too many players could hit the ball, because I threw so hard and fast, and I could put the ball anywhere I wanted. Ronnie would set up on the outside, and I threw it out there. Everywhere his mitt went, I landed a ball there. And let's face it, not too many eight-year-olds could consistently throw a strike to begin with. I felt like a baseball god!

I knew I was good, but it felt great for other people to see it too. "Let's go, Big Pete! Strike this guy out!" my teammates would encourage me, using a nickname they'd given me because of my size. The opposing team's players also noticed I was good. I could tell by the way the batters would approach home base and stare almost fearfully at me, just waiting and knowing that the word *strike* was coming . . . and then the word *strikeout.* Coaches noticed, parents noticed, everybody noticed my talent.

But not all of them believed I was that good and only an eight-year-old. Because I was such a big kid, folks began murmuring that maybe I wasn't as young as I claimed to be. "Where's his birth certificate?" they'd complain. "There's no way that Big Pete kid is eight years old."

I tried not to listen to what people were saying, but their comments, along with my ever-growing height and weight, began to chisel away at my confidence. At a time when I should have been carefree and innocent, my self-doubt took over, and I became a scared, insecure kid. And my too-tight uniform only proved the truth of who I began to believe I was—not a talented ball player, but a fat one.

• • •

It's amazing how even as children, we can twist things around and begin to believe "facts" about ourselves that aren't true, but they stick with us and play out as though they *are* true. As a child, I was bigger, stronger, and taller than most kids my age. I was well aware of this, and was reminded simply by my nickname, "Big Pete." My size was an issue I'd dealt with from before I could even remember.

When I was two years old, I was growing so fast that Mom and Dad became concerned and took me to a specialist in Navasota, which was twenty-five miles from Brenham. The pediatrician there ordered special blood tests to determine what was causing the growth spurt. The test results came back normal, so he told my parents to decrease and monitor my food intake. "He's going to be a big man. He has big bones," the doctor concluded.

At *two*, I was put on a diet.

Easier said than done, though. I *wanted* food, and if I didn't get it, even at that young age, I would throw a temper tantrum. I would sit in my high chair and scream and cry and beat on the chair's tray until they finally grew tired of dealing with it and gave in to my demands.

More than anything else, I remember people always talking about me losing weight. Over and over I heard, "You need to watch what you eat" and "You don't need any more food." I felt as though everyone was determined to beat it into my head. I wanted to shout, "I heard you the first time—loud and clear. Your words have not fallen on deaf ears!"

Part of the problem was simply that I loved to eat, and I ate a lot. If someone put food in front of me, that food usually didn't last long. I could suck it up like a Hoover vacuum. People would often tell me, "Slow down. Chew your food. That food doesn't have legs, it ain't going anywhere!" But I just couldn't. I had no stop button, and it didn't help that my mom was such a great cook.

Almost every night, our family gathered around the kitchen table to eat supper together. Mom usually prepared a large meal—enough to feed our family of four and then the rest of the county. Pork chops, meatloaf, beef goulash, pot roast, ribeyes, sirloins, chicken fingers. My favorite was when Mom made chicken fried steak smothered in cream gravy. It was all about the batter—the more breaded the meat, the better. Double- or triple-dipping the meat in eggs and flour, Mom created that special and thick outer layer.

Added to that, we always had a fresh baked loaf of bread or rolls with a mountain of butter, and two or three side dishes, one of which was usually broccoli. My dad often said with a chuckle, "If broccoli causes cancer, we're sure to get it." But overeating broccoli clearly wasn't my problem.

I lacked discipline in pushing away from the table when I was full, and instead of eating just one plate of food, I usually got seconds, and sometimes thirds, cleaning off those plates as well.

That kind of eating came with a price, though. I endured constant comments about my weight, which settled into my soul, accusing me constantly of being fat, of being ugly . . . of being no good.

So when some parent or coach from another team accused me of being older than eight, it bothered me, because it was just another reminder that I wasn't like everybody else, that I was cheating or bad in some way. Mom and Dad would try to brush it off with, "They're just upset because of how good you are. They talk about the birth certificate because you're so tall and strong." Regardless, it still bothered me.

I looked in the mirror and saw what they saw: a big, tall, broad-shouldered, fat kid.

Throughout practices I could ignore my size. We were all friends, teammates—all working hard and trying to be the best we could be for our team. We depended on one another. Other than calling me Big Pete, I really didn't sense they were trying to be mean.

It was more the clothing that was the problem. One of the best parts of practice was that we wore what we wanted—our own comfortable clothes that allowed us to move freely without any restrictions. But games were different. Pee Wee Little League provided uniforms they expected us to wear.

We all wore short-sleeved, maroon mesh shirts, similar to the texture of typical basketball shirts, with white *Yankees* lettering ironed across the front and our numbers ironed on the back, which all eventually peeled and flaked off after being washed and dried repeatedly. We all also had maroon-and-white breathable, adjustable hats. But each player supplied the rest of his uniform—from the socks to the plastic-cleated shoes—although some boys just wore sneakers—to the blue jean pants.

Although I never complained or made it known, I hated wearing those pants. I could never find the right size to fit me well, and they were extremely tight and restrictive, causing me to move around like a robot in a stiff, awkward, and clumsy way without any flexibility or freedom. I had to suck in my stomach in order to button and zip them up. And once I had them on, my legs and my butt felt like an inner tube blown up by a high-pressure air compressor. I was over-inflated by a lot of pounds.

Usually during the games, I'd figured out how to maneuver to be the least obvious of how uncomfortable they were. But during one particular game, my pants gave me away.

I was up to bat, and the pitcher had thrown four straight balls. Although in a regular game, four balls meant I could walk to first base, in Pee Wee Little League, the rules called for the batter to hit off a tee. They wanted to prevent a "walk-a-thon," since pitchers that age would more easily walk hitter after hitter than strike anybody out. It was a way to allow all the players an opportunity to hit while also allowing the defense to make some plays. The batter would then have three chances to swing and put the ball into play.

Hitting off the tee was okay, but I preferred to hit live pitching. The ball seemed to travel farther when I hit off of the pitcher. The tee was boring; I liked action.

So the umpire called, "Ball four" and I stepped out of the right-handed batters' box, adjusted the batting glove on my hand, and took a few practice swings as the umpire set up the tee. I had hit a few homeruns off the tee that season, and of course, I was trying to go "deep" again, and hit it far into the outfield. If I made good contact and got the ball up in the air, it had a good chance of clearing the fences. The opposing players must have figured out my strategy because they all stepped back from their normal positions, anticipating that I would hit the ball hard.

"Okay," the umpire said and signaled for me to step in to swing.

Returning to the batter's box and holding the bat with a firm, tight grip, I took another few practice swings to align the bat with the ball. Because of the lack of rain and hot temperatures that summer, the batter's box was as hard as concrete and covered with loose, gritty dirt. It was like standing on an ice rink and wearing roller blades instead of ice skates. I tried several times to adjust my shoes to find some traction and to get a comfortable and steady feel.

With all my strength, I cocked the bat back, lifted my front leg, and swung as hard as I could, as though trying to rip the cover off the ball. But instead of hearing a *ting* from making contact, the only sound I heard was a dull, bat-stopping *thug*. I'd missed completely, hitting the rubber tee a few inches beneath the ball.

As the tee fell forward and the ball fell and dribbled away from home plate, my feet began slipping on the tiny grains of dirt and my body continued to twist. Without any grace or coordination, my body flailed as I lost all sense of balance. Spinning around in a one-eighty degree turn, I fell down face-first in the batter's box.

Scrambling to get up to brush the dirt off my pants and shirt before anyone noticed, I pushed myself up to swing again.

But I'd been too slow. I had *not* gone unnoticed.

The laughter started, first coming from both dugouts, and then, horrifically, from some of the parents in the bleachers. It was as though someone had pressed the slow-motion button on a remote to make sure no one missed any of the action. The laughter grew louder as embarrassment and shame consumed me.

I had to save face. I had to act as though what had just happened was completely routine and normal, that maybe I'd even meant it to happen. So I decided to pretend it was no big deal. I swept the dirt from my pants and shirt and stepped up to the tee again, which the umpire had reset.

Just as I positioned myself to swing a second time, I realized something was seriously wrong. My pants had come unbuttoned, and if I didn't button them, my zipper would work its way down with every movement. There was no way I could run like that when I hit the ball, and I was not taking the chance of my pants falling down.

I had no other choice; I'd have to rebutton my pants.

Please, please, don't watch me now, I silently begged, feeling everyone's eyes on me.

I placed the bat on the ground and sucked in my stomach to button my pants. I could hear the laughter start up again as the crowd realized what I was doing.

"Some swing, batter boy!" someone yelled from the opposing team's side. "He went and popped his pants!"

My fingers slipped and no matter how many times I tried, the pants refused to button. The button seemed to get more and more rigid. Because of my batting glove, I couldn't get a good grip on the button, and it kept slipping out of my fingers. With every slip of the button, more tears welled up in my eyes and my heart sank lower. And the crowd laughed and laughed, each one echoing in my eight-year-old ears.

Finally, with fumbling hands I pulled my zipper up as tight as I could get it, leaving the button undone, tried to cover everything over by slightly pulling out my shirt, and picked my bat back up.

I quickly swung two more times, determined not to hit the ball or the tee, and then I walked back to the dugout with my head down. The walk seemed to take forever, and although I didn't want any of the attention, I could feel the stares. With every step I took, their laughter became louder and louder, as though the volume of a microphone in my head had been turned up all the way. Their laughter sent very clear messages:

I'm fat.

I'm worthless.

I'm not good enough.

I don't fit in.

I can't play baseball.

No matter how fast I could pitch or how great I played, it couldn't overcome the truth of that laughter, the truth of all the dieting comments in my life. They knew who I was. And at eight years old, I believed them.

CHAPTER 4
"I WANT TO QUIT!"

I adjusted my cap and looked at my catcher, Neal Pieper. He was squatting behind home plate with his glove facing me, ready to catch and end the inning. This was an important inning for us. The score was tied and the potential winning run was standing on third base. If the runner made it home, we were finished.

I wound up and threw the pitch as fast as I could. The batter swung, popping the ball up high in the air. An easy catch. An easy out.

The right fielder ran in with his glove aimed toward the ball, and he missed it. The runner took off like a bullet and tromped right over home base.

"Safe!" the umpire yelled and pushed his arms straight out from his sides.

And that was that. The game was over and the Red Sox had lost. *We'd* lost. Again.

I grabbed the baseball with my bare hand and threw it as far as I could toward right field and huffed loudly. I was so sick of losing.

For two years, when I was eight and nine, my teams did extremely well, and I was the show-off kid, pitching and winning. Then I graduated from Pee Wee to Minor Little League and I fully expected the winning streak to continue.

Winning had become the norm for me. Seldom had I experienced losing, and if our team did lose, it happened at the end of the season when our team had already clinched first place, which meant it was really no big deal in my mind. No one remembers the details of one game anyway. They remember the team crowned champion, right?

But this season, nothing seemed to go our way. My teammates were all good guys and played all-out, always giving their best efforts. But our follow-through wasn't there and we just couldn't get it together. The hits, the catches, the runs—they'd vanish when we needed them the most. We would start winning, then someone on the team would make an error, and the other team would come back and win. Loss after loss after loss had now become the expected outcome for the Red Sox.

I hated it. Losing wasn't fun. It was bad enough that I still dealt with the size issue. I was so much bigger than the others on my team that I had to have a special uniform made for me, because none of the league-issued shirts fit me. As embarrassing as that had been, though, at least baseball had been a stable force for me. We won; I felt confident. So often it was the score rather than my performance that dictated my mood. Winning reflected success, while losing was synonymous with failure. And since I believed the way I was viewed was important, winning was critical.

I wanted others, specifically my parents, coaches, and teammates, to think I was one of the best. And when I believed they didn't think that way—because we kept losing at baseball—that thought was troubling to me. With this season as we piled up the losses, doubts of my ability started popping around in my head like kernels of corn being heated and ready to explode. It was not just that we'd lost; it was that *I* was a loser.

Finally, after this loss, I'd had enough.

As my dad, who was now my coach, packed up and everyone talked over the game, I grabbed my glove and bat and walked to his truck, got in, and sat. The thick southern Texas air hung heavy and felt suffocating in the truck. But I didn't notice and didn't much care; the continual losses were the only thing on my mind.

I've disappointed Dad. I've disappointed everybody. Why can't I win? My mind jabbed and accused me over and over. *Failure, failure, failure.*

After about fifteen minutes, Dad threw the equipment into the back of the pickup's cab, slid quietly behind the steering wheel, and directed the Ford toward home.

I was so upset I couldn't even say anything. I just felt dejected. All I wanted was to go home, take a shower, and head to bed. I wanted to be left alone, away from any talk or any questions. Or worse, any pity. I knew they were all thinking what a loser I was. It wasn't just the game; it was me as a person. As I replayed the game in my mind, I thought about what our team could have done differently.

In Texas, we're told that real men are tough; they don't cry. So my life seemed even worse when tears welled up in my eyes and I couldn't seem to stop them. I'd tried so long to keep it in, to be tough. My lips pressed together and I blinked hard.

Don't cry, I kept telling myself, as the tears multiplied. My breathing became heavier and I tried to breathe through my nose, but now snot mixed with the tears. I was a mess and I had no idea what to do about it, other than to keep trying to fight against it.

The tears won—I'd even lost against that! As they began to flow freely down my face, I put my head down and turned away, pretending to look out the passenger window. I'd tried with all my might to hold it in, but I was failing.

"I want to quit." I said the words quietly but loud enough for my dad to hear them over the rumble of the truck's engine and the hot wind blasting through the open windows. "I'm not having fun anymore."

With that admission, the flood gates burst and I started to sob. Deep, heavy, aching moans erupted from my lips as tears splashed down on my specially-made uniform creating big wet splotches all over my shirt.

I wiped my nose with my hand and sat there hiccupping and heaving.

Dad didn't respond right away. He let my sobs fill the Ford until slowly my tears began to subside. "It's okay to let it out, Jon," he said in a kind and loving tone. "I believe in you. Just hang in there, and together we'll get through this season. That's a promise, okay? I love you, son."

A second round of spasming waterworks rushed over my face again. He knew what I was going through. He didn't like losing either. And more important, I knew he had my back. He wanted us to win just as much as I did.

He isn't disappointed in me, I realized. I wasn't alone. He believed in me and I didn't have to be a tough guy. My winning a baseball game didn't correlate with the amount of love he had for me.

I nodded and sniffed. I still didn't like losing. I still wasn't thrilled over the prospect that we may continue losing for the rest of the season, but somehow, my dad's words lifted a burden off me. It wasn't my fault. Things would be okay. Everything would turn out just fine.

● ● ●

I wish I could have remembered that important lesson, but my skull was a little too thick. The saying goes, "He's getting too big for his britches."

The saying was true of me—and not just literally, because my size meant that none of the uniforms fit me and I had to have a special uniform sewn just for me. No, my attitude, craziness, and temper had gotten out of control.

My dad had been correct and that season everything did turn out okay. I stuck with playing, and though our team didn't do much better, I kept my head down, gave my best effort, and looked forward to the following year when I'd move up to big Little League, have new teammates, and a new start.

What a difference a year made! My dad was still my coach and I was now on the Indians. Our team was excellent, finishing the season with a record of 16-2—sixteen wins and two losses. And my pitching record was 8-1—eight wins and one loss. I even hit eleven homeruns. We played hard and won. To make baseball life even better, I was one of only four eleven-year-olds selected to the All-Star team. We were eliminated in the first tournament, but I didn't care. I was getting better and having fun again.

The next season, my dad decided to step away from coaching and be a spectator. He wanted to have time to watch not only me, but also my brother. And with work and caring for our home on twenty acres, he couldn't be in all places. That didn't mean he stopped giving me little pointers, though: "Slow down your windup some"; "Make sure you get good balance"; "Try different grips on the ball."

Many of the boys were my age so they returned to our team, plus we added a few new players. Our coaches were new too. Chester Markwardt and Randy Markwardt may have been brothers but they seemed as different as night and day. Chester, our head coach, whose son, Brian, was new to our team, was the serious, stricter one. Randy, our assistant coach, was more like me, playing around all the time and cracking jokes. Randy had pitched at Baylor University. Though he didn't have any sons, he'd volunteered to help out because of his love of kids and the game.

I was thrilled! *A guy who pitched in college is going to coach me.* I thought. *I'm really good now, just wait until he gets a hold of me!*

The season went on just as expected. Our team was really good, often beating teams by ten runs or more. We were unstoppable. And I was overbearing on the mound, throwing the ball so hard and fast that not many boys could hit it. I felt as if I were on top of the world again—as long as everything went my way.

With only two games left in our season, we knew we were going to dominate the league. So by that penultimate game, on June 8, 1983, I was cocky and ready to go. We were playing against the Braves, and I was on the mound. By now I'd earned an impressive reputation, and when the opposing team came against me to bat, they looked a little as though they wanted to run home to Mommy. It was as if they knew they were beaten beforehand and they had no reason even to try.

The 6:00 p.m. game had just started, and I struck out the first two batters with no trouble. (We were the home team.) With one more out, we'd be hitting.

"Three up, three down! You got this, Jon," my mom yelled from the first-base-side bleachers.

My good friend Eddie Marshall now stood before me, squinting and looking determined. He was a bigger and stronger kid, like me, and very athletic. I peered at Neal, our returning catcher from last season. With his right hand between his legs, he signaled with his index finger, "Number One—Fastball." I nodded, rubbed the ball around in my glove, wound up, and let the ball go flying straight toward his glove. Only, Eddie swung hard and hit the ball. Up, up, and far out to center field it headed. I watched the ball sail into the air. *Don't go over! Come down! No! Please come back!* I pleaded silently as I watched the ball float at a turtle's pace. Landing somewhere over the chain-link fenced boundaries of the field, he'd done what no one else had *ever* done against me—hit a homerun.

The opposing team's fans went crazy with whooping and cheering. As Eddie pumped his fist in the air and raced around the diamond, touching each base as he went, my blood pressure soared and my face felt as if it were an inferno.

That wasn't even a good hit! I yelled in my mind. *Just a little check swing. He didn't even really swing at it! He was just lucky!*

I started stomping all over the mound, kicking dirt, and huffing and puffing. My face throbbed from the heat of my fury, and I kept mumbling, "That wasn't even a good hit!"

Out to the mound walked Coach Randy. He had a laid back, good-ole-boy mentality, laughing and having fun a lot, although he would get serious when he needed to. At this moment, I was in no mood to hear jokes; I was in no mood to hear *anything*.

"Jon, it's okay," he told me, obviously trying to get me to calm down. "It's just one run, and we have six innings to score runs. It's not that big of a deal."

Not that big of a deal? I would have decked him if I wouldn't have been thrown out of baseball for life. There was no calming me down, and the game came to a halt while everyone watched me have a meltdown on the field.

"Come on, now," Coach continued. "Eddie's your friend. You should be happy he was able to do what nobody else has done. Wouldn't you want him to be happy if it were you getting that homerun?"

"I don't care that he's my friend." And I didn't. He'd committed the cardinal sin: he'd hit a homerun off one of my pitches. I was bound and determined not to let that happen again.

Eventually, I regained my composure and I pitched with a fervor for the rest of the game. The next time Eddie was up to bat, I threw as hard as I could and struck him out, *one, two, three*—quick as a flash. And our team went on to win the game—Indians 12, Braves 2 (*It should have only been 1*, I kept mumbling to myself).

We finished the season 17-1, and as a pitcher I was 8-0. But that wasn't good enough. I hated that Eddie had broken my clean record and nailed that homerun off one of my pitches.

• • •

A lot of people attributed my temper flare ups to being a byproduct of adolescence, but I knew the truth. I was deeply insecure and angry. Even though everything looked great in my life—I was killing it in baseball and I was a star on the basketball team—I felt empty inside. Everybody had eyes on the Peters kid, who was going to do great things. But I felt like a fake. I was sure they'd discover the truth about me: that I was no good. The "hole in my soul" was real, and I didn't know how to handle it or communicate what I was feeling. I didn't even know *what* exactly I was feeling! I just knew I was miserable. On the field, as long as we won, as long as I did well on the mound, then everything felt stable and okay for the moment. But off the field, or if we weren't doing quite as well as I expected, my anger seethed.

Mostly I took it out on my family and those friends who were closest to me. The temper tantrums I'd had over food when I was two grew into monster tantrums over *everything* with each passing year. I sassed, I told my parents to shut up, I rolled my eyes, I cussed them out. I threw things, I broke windows. I was nasty and cruel.

It wasn't right, but in my mind, I desperately wanted some boundaries. It didn't matter what I said or did, I never received any punishment. It felt sort of like a free-for-all. I demanded things of my parents, and to keep the peace—and probably because they didn't know how to handle the monster within—they gave in. But that only made me more angry and disrespectful. And I could go from zero to one hundred fast— for no reason at all. Just as I had no control over my eating, I had no control over my anger—at least where my parents were concerned.

For instance, one year while we were at Henderson Field watching a Big League All-Star game, in which the sixteen- through eighteen-year-olds played, it was "Pass the Hat" time. Pass the Hat was a call for donations to help the Little League program. Instead of passing an actual hat, several half-gallon Blue Bell Ice Cream containers would float around the bleachers for people to drop in cash as they desired. My dad was overseeing one bleacher section and asked me to help with another section. It required me to stand in front of the bleachers, and after the spectators had their opportunity to contribute, I'd collect the donations and take the container to him. I didn't want to do that.

"Jon, will you handle that section?" my dad asked, pointing to the section to his right where we'd been sitting.

"Nope," I quickly answered.

Standing on a mound and having people look at me while I was pitching was one thing. I felt in control and I knew I could pitch. Standing in front of a crowd and asking for money scared me to death. I was certain I would sound stupid, and the crowd would make fun of me for being fat and ugly. But instead of telling my dad I felt that way, I chose the less mature way and caused a scene—that way I could insure I wouldn't have to participate and I wouldn't have to tell them who I really was. I could keep the secret of what I thought about myself.

"Please?" he said in a nice but pleading way. "Can you just go pass the hat? I really need your help in collecting all the containers."

"I said *no*! I don't want to do it! And I'm *not* going to do it."

"Jon, you're *going* to pass the hat. Now go do it," Dad replied with a stern, commanding voice.

By this time, the people who were sitting around me in the bleachers noticed our conversation. They slowly began turning their heads toward me, listening to our exchange. I began to creatively hear in my imaginative mind: *Just go help your dad, Jon. What a spoiled little brat! If you were my kid, it wouldn't be good when we got home.*

I shouted the worst expletive and then told him to leave me alone. The one thing I'd wanted—to avoid attention—I now had in spades. Every eye in the bleachers was staring at me. I stood and walked off the bleachers in a hurry. I knew I had to move quickly because he would be right after me and catch me. He wore boots all the time, but he was fast.

I sprinted a few hundred yards across a vacant field toward Fireman's Park, where another baseball game was being played. Our car was parked over there because we'd planned on watching games at both fields, switching from one to the other. As I ran, I looked back over my shoulder to see if my dad was coming after me. Sure enough, he was on his way and he was gaining ground, getting closer with each stride.

I can't let him catch me, no way. I know he'll take off his belt and whip me. What am I going to do? Why can't he just leave me alone? I'm not sure why I was worried about getting a whipping—Dad did it a few times, but it never did any good in changing my behavior; in fact, it only made me angrier and nastier, so he stopped.

Panicking and knowing he'd catch me eventually, I stopped right in the middle of the one busy street that ran between the two fields. Looking back and making eye contact with him, I yelled, "Hey, Dad, if you come one step farther. . . . See that car?" I pointed to an oncoming vehicle. "I'm going to step right out in front of it."

He froze immediately. Maybe he thought I was actually going to do it. Once the car passed, I ran and hurriedly slid into our car and locked the doors.

I'm safe now. Hopefully Dad will calm down and forget about it.

When Dad saw that I wasn't coming out, and since he had to get back to collecting the containers, he finally left. I sat in that hot car, dripping sweat from the Texas heat, glad I'd escaped my dad. I knew the anger would pass, and my family would never confront me or talk about it. I didn't relish possibly getting into trouble, but something inside me wanted boundaries and a sense of knowing that I was okay. Even though I didn't know how to express myself better and articulate why I did what I did, I desperately wanted someone to tell me that the crazy stuff I believed about myself—that I was stupid and fat and ugly—wasn't true.

But my family never did. Even though they told me they loved me, that hole in my soul was just too deep for them to fill.

● ● ●

Faith didn't even seem to help. Every Sunday my family and I would head to church. Sometimes during the singing or a particular sermon, I'd feel something moving inside me, nudging me with the truth of the message. I liked that; it was calming. But mostly, church and God were strictly a Sunday-morning-only ordeal I had to put up with.

Then one year during this time, Billy Graham brought his famous crusade to Blinn College, not far from our house in Brenham. Mom, my brother, and I attended every night. At the end of each service, they'd sing a hymn and offer an "altar call," a time for people to respond to the message by walking forward and praying to accept Jesus into their lives.

At the end of each night, they would sing the old hymn by Charlotte Elliott, "Just as I Am."

> Just as I am, without one plea,
> But that Thy blood was shed for me,
> And that Thou bidst me come to Thee,
> O Lamb of God, I come. I come.

The music was soothing, and once again, I felt something stir within me.

Mom nudged me. "Hey, Jon, let's go up there, and you give your life to Christ. How does that sound?"

I didn't really know what it was all about, but I felt emotionally moved, plus it looked interesting, and I was always game for adventure, so I agreed.

We moved through the crowds until we got to the front of the stadium. Mom gently pushed me toward one of the volunteers, who talked to me about Jesus' death for my sins, and how when I accept him, I'll have a new life, a different life.

That sounded good to me. I wanted a life in which I didn't feel so insecure or empty any more. Where I didn't deal with anger issues or the insecurities of being a fake and a failure. I wanted peace.

When the volunteer asked if I was ready to accept Jesus into my heart, I said yes.

Mom was pleased. But I didn't feel any different.

So I went back home and looked forward to what I knew brought real pleasure and peace: baseball. And I was getting better at it all the time.

CHAPTER 5
FIRST TASTE OF FAME

"You made it! You're on the team!" my dad called out late one afternoon toward the end of my Little League season. "You made the All-Stars."

"Woohoo!" I cheered with a fist pump and ran into the kitchen where Dad had just gotten off the phone with the All-Star coach, Chester Markwardt. I felt as if I had made it to the Big Time. Only fourteen players got chosen for the All-Star team. In a small town, you'd think that wasn't so big a deal—that it would be easy to make that team. But not in Brenham, Texas, where *every* kid was a competitor, and where baseball ran through everybody's veins. Baseball isn't just in the water, as some people would joke; it's in our DNA. And at twelve years old, I was no exception. Similar to red cells, white cells, and platelets, fastballs, curveballs, and changeups flowed through my bloodstream.

With the All-Star team, we would first play teams from surrounding counties in the area tournament, and if we won, we would advance to district, and then to sectionals, and then to state. If we took state, we would head to regionals, then off to the Little League World Series—the big shindig, with teams from all around the world. This year it would be in Williamsport, Pennsylvania. I knew we were going to win it all. I just *knew* it. Especially because we had a killer team. I was already friends with most of the boys and we had either played together or against one another long enough to know our strengths and how to work well together.

Our first game was in July 1983 against Giddings. Giddings was about forty-five minutes northwest, halfway between Brenham and Austin. Every All-Star season, the area tournament would alternate game locations among the teams in the surrounding counties to eliminate any "unfair" advantage. This year, we played in Navasota, just thirty minutes down the road from us on Highway 105. The Giddings team had a good fan turn out, but nothing like ours. I think our entire community shut down whatever they were doing and headed to Navasota to watch us play.

"How are you doing, Jon?" Coach Markwardt asked me as our team was warming up.

"Okay. Doing good," I replied, but actually feeling anxious.

"Good." Coach nodded. I could tell he wanted to win this game as much as I did. Our reputation was on the line. No way could *Brenham not* advance beyond the first round. With the talent we had, that just wasn't an option.

The top of the first inning set the tone for the evening. We jumped on the Giddings starting pitcher for an early three-run lead. When I was up to bat, I scorched a single hard up the middle. Then for the bottom of the inning, I was on the mound, ready to start my first All-Star game as a pitcher. My stomach felt jittery, and I tried to shake off the nerves. I'd played in front of crowds since I was eight. But this felt different. It was more important. It was my time to shine.

The first batter approached home plate, and after a quick three strikes, he made his way back to the dugout.

The same happened to the second batter. And the third.

Three up, three down. End of inning one. Brenham 3, Giddings 0.

When it was my time to bat again, I stepped up to home plate, took a few practice swings, and focused my eyes on the pitcher. I watched as he wound up, pulled the ball from his glove, and sent it reeling right toward me. I inhaled deeply, kept my eyes glued on the ball, and swung as hard I could. It looked like a colorless cantaloupe with a tattooed bullseye floating in the air, big and slow, that was saying, *Hit me! Hit me right here!*

Crack!

The ball went flying high and deep over the infielders' and outfielders' heads. There was no way that ball was staying in the park. I'd gotten all of it. It was not a question of it going over the fence; rather the question was, by how far. It cleared the fence at the top of the field's lights, and traveled over cars and trucks that were parked some fifteen to twenty yards beyond the left field fence. And with bases loaded, it was a grand slam!

I threw down my bat, jogged the first base line, and watched the ball go and go. I'd never hit a ball so far. As I rounded the bases, I noticed the infielders glaring out into the left field distance. Their pale, blank stares said it all, *We're done. This Brenham team is way too good for us.* They quickly moved out of my way when I got closer to them. Compared to me, they looked like babies who were at least a foot shorter. Finally, I made it to home plate, where I stepped hard right on the plate without breaking a sweat.

My teammates high-fived and patted me on the back when I returned to the dugout. The Brenham fans stood, clapped, and hooted and hollered.

"Way to go, Big Pete!" one of the fans yelled.

"Wow! You hit that ball a mile!" a teammate shouted.

Several other players crossed home plate that inning, making the score eight to zero. And while I was excited to watch them add runs, I kept thinking, *I can really do this! I'm playing the best of the best players, and I'm striking them out and hitting homeruns! Maybe I am pretty good?*

At the bottom of the inning, I grabbed my glove and headed back out to the mound. Once again, the first batter up quickly struck out. Then the second. Then the third. That was six batters in a row I'd just taken down!

The next time I was up to bat—*crack!*—another homerun. Another monster shot, but this time to right center.

And the next time I pitched? Another three quick strike-outs. End of three innings played. Nine Giddings batters, nine strikeouts. Brenham 12, Giddings 0.

Over and over, each inning was the same. I couldn't believe how on fire I was. I could do no wrong. It seemed as if the rest of my teammates walked onto the field, counted to ten, and walked right back off so we could score more runs!

I added a third homerun to my stats that game. But more importantly, I struck out every batter who came to the plate, holding his bat, and waiting for me to pitch. There were no hits, no walks, no runs, and no errors—a perfect game. I over-powered the hitters with my fastball and dazzled them with my control. The catcher didn't have to move much that day; wherever he put his mitt, I put the ball. It was like throwing darts and hitting the bullseye every time. Eighteen strikeouts out of eighteen hitters in all for a perfect 20-0 victory.

I was riding high the whole trip back to Brenham as I knew this was our first step toward becoming Little League World Series champions.

Brrring. Brrring. Once home, our phone rang nonstop. Friends and people in the community called to congratulate me and cheer me on. But now, added to those well-wishers, were a new group of callers: reporters looking to get a quote from me. Mom or Dad would hand me the phone and tell me who was on the other end of the call. They'd always encourage me to say something positive about the team—which was easy to do, since I knew the whole team won the game, not just me.

I felt awkward talking about myself. Being on the field and being cocky was one thing, but being asked to be cocky on command was quite another. So basically, I just reiterated each time that I loved the game, had fun, enjoyed my teammates and coaches, and just tried to do the best I could. That always seemed to appease the people interviewing me.

After I got off the phone, though, I didn't think much more about it. I didn't know why they wanted to talk to me or what they were going to do with what I said. I found out soon enough.

Our local newspaper, *The Banner Press*, as well as a few of the other surrounding cities' newspapers—the *Bryan-College Station Eagle*, the *San Antonio Light,* the *Houston Chronicle*, and the *Houston Post*—did write-ups on the game and my shut-out performance. Each paper included my name with my photo and that I'd pitched a perfect game striking out eighteen of eighteen batters.

Now it seemed as though everywhere I went, somebody would yell out about that game and what a good player I was. It was the first time I experienced publicity, and I thought it was somewhat fun. My mom picked up copies of every news article, carefully clipped each out, and pasted it into a scrapbook. With every report, she'd exclaim, "Look, Jon, they mention you here," or "Here's another one, Jon!"

A day or so after the local papers released, Mom and I were in the kitchen and I was eating a snack when the phone rang. Mom answered cheerily and as she listened to the person on the other end, her eyes grew large. "You're kidding," she said. "Really?" They talked a few moments more and then Mom hung up.

"Jon, what you did got picked up by the *Wall Street Journal* and the *New York Times!*" Being only twelve, I wasn't sure exactly how big a deal that was, but I could tell it was something special from the excitement in her voice and from the size of her eyes.

In my mind, as long as I kept playing and winning, I didn't really care who covered it!

And our team *did* keep playing and winning. And now, more and more reporters and photographers were showing up, not just to report on the game, but to keep an eye on the twelve-year-old kid who'd pitched a perfect game. I wished I could have thrown a perfect game every time, but I only got that one. Even so, we still won against all the other local teams, then the district and sectional teams, and finally we made it to state, where we did well but not good enough.

Although I was sad that we didn't make it to the Little League World Series, the experience relit that fire in my belly and made it even stronger than it had ever been—and I was determined that I *would* make it there.

Even with all the accolades and the taste of publicity and fame, though, I still struggled with the insecurity of my size and ability. You see, I was five feet, ten inches, and weighed 165 pounds. I was taller and heavier than all the players. And yes, I was even taller than my coach. And I was *twelve*.

Even the reporters made comments about it. One wrote, "He's larger than a lot of the players whom his brother Ronnie plays with on the Brenham High School varsity team." It didn't matter that the reporter also wrote, "[He] averages fifteen strikeouts a game out of a possible eighteen." What mattered was that the reporter not only noticed my tender spot, but spotlighted it, and then even quoted my mom: "People are always questioning his age." The reporter continued, "The size difference does not go unnoticed by All-Star opponents meeting Peters for the first time. The doctor said, 'He has a big bone structure.' Ruth said, 'He just towers over everyone.'"

What should have been a great write-up still poked at my insecurities. So I kept working hard, hoping I could *play* my way out of feeling so insecure and different from everybody else.

• • •

The following year our hard work paid off—we were headed to Taylor, Michigan, to compete in the Junior Little League World Series! I made the All-Stars again—and this time, we went all the way, winning state, and now focusing on taking the whole thing.

Our team had a blast together—we spent the summer traveling, laughing, joking around, and of course, playing a lot of baseball. I often thought, *I'm the luckiest kid in the world*.

My size even seemed to get under control. By the time I hit thirteen, my growth slowed down and some of the other kids started to catch up to me. I was still bigger but we were becoming closer in size. And in good time too; I didn't think I could handle another season of someone wondering loudly or complaining that my presence on the team was illegal because I was older than the others.

The thing is, when you carry around people's comments and those skewed perspectives about yourself, even when things change, that perspective doesn't necessarily go out the window. Although my size wasn't as noticeable or something many people commented on anymore, I still carried the shame and pain of the past. I still felt as if I were that eight-year-old, innocent boy with the tight jeans that unbuttoned and caused everybody to laugh. I was still big-boned, big-eating "Big Pete." I still believed that people thought I was fat and not good enough. I could look at myself in a mirror and rather than see the truth of the image there—a normal-sized, normal-looking kid—I still saw that chubby, awkward, out-of-place boy. And I still ached over it and lashed out based on who I saw and felt myself to be. I clung to the cockiness of my ability on the field, always praying and hoping that it would continue to be enough.

Now heading to the World Series, I figured this was my opportunity to show the world that I wasn't who I believed they all thought I was. And I was going to prove it by winning. I knew no other way.

Our team and many of the parents flew to Detroit and then drove to Taylor, one of Detroit's suburbs. I couldn't wait to see the field and the beautiful scenery surrounding it. I thought, *This is the World Series. We're going to play in a beautiful place. This is going to be top notch!* I figured the field would sit in the middle of nice subdivisions with big, expensive homes. But as we drove to the field, I kept wondering if perhaps we'd taken the wrong turn and gotten lost. The neighborhoods we passed through were dumpy and scary looking. Trash and filth seemed to be everywhere. Vacant, dilapidated buildings boarded up. Empty lots and rusty, broken-down cars. And then we drove into an industrial section, where we passed big, gray, dingy factories and large parking lots that hadn't been paved in decades.

This can't be the place. I thought. *This is the dumps. This isn't what we signed up for.*

I couldn't understand how we had ended up here. The World Series was supposed to be the cream of the crop, so to my way of thinking, the host city should be too—especially since a dozen or so teams from all over the world were going here to compete.

I tried to shrug it off. *It doesn't really matter*, I told myself. *I'm not here to sightsee, anyway. Our team has a title to win.*

We played good and hard and won most of the games. But when it came down to it, we ended up in third place, losing to the teams from Pearl City, Hawaii (in first place), and Wilmington, Delaware (in second). We'd actually beaten Wilmington in the tournament, but they beat us during the final rounds.

Everybody still applauded us and told us how well we did and how close we'd come to winning, but they didn't understand: third place was not the same as first place. Third place didn't get you anywhere. Third place still lost.

I knew I should have been happy about the experience and finishing how we had, but I was more comfortable sulking about it. If I'd done better; if we'd worked harder . . . Everything in my brain told me *if, if, if* . . . then we would have won.

That unhappy void appeared in my life and soul again. And I wasn't sure how to overcome it.

CHAPTER 6
COACH DRIGGERS

There was a new coach in town. And he was all anybody was talking about. Lee Driggers had been drafted as a pitcher by the Los Angeles Dodgers in the late 1960s and had played minor league baseball in the Pioneer and Florida State leagues before turning his sights to coaching. Prior to taking over at the helm of the baseball program in Brenham, he had coached for several years, most recently as the head coach at Willowridge High School in Houston.

I had read about him in the newspaper and had heard about him through the local gossip, but that was it. I was interested in what was going on in the town, especially when it came to baseball, but at the time, my focus was more on playing ball with the All-Stars. Plus, I was only going to be an eighth grader so I figured our paths would probably not cross for a year.

My parents attended every game. Come hell or high water, they were not going to miss one inning. My mom sat in the bleachers hootin' and hollerin' with the other mothers, while my dad, along with the other fathers, stood near our team's dugout watching every pitch. They never talked to me during the games, never interfered with the coaching, and never offered suggestions, though. So I was surprised during our game against Tyler North in the sectional tournament at Fireman's Park in Brenham when, around the fourth inning, Dad approached the dugout. That wasn't like him at all, so I thought, *This must be something important.*

"Coach Driggers said to change speeds and mix the location of the pitches more often," Dad whispered through the chain-link fence. I was having a tough time striking out the batters because they kept making a lot of contact, although most of the time they fouled the ball off. They were "free-swingers," which meant they would swing at anything. And since I was always throwing pitches around the strike zone, they would hit at times. I was working hard trying to overpower them, and I was feeling exhausted. Maybe Coach Driggers thought I was using all my energy.

"Okay," I said quickly and walked back to the front of the dugout where I was standing with my teammates.

I was confused, but after thinking about what he said, I agreed. *But why? Why would someone I have never met offer those suggestions?* I couldn't even pick him out of a line up! But from what I had heard about him, I knew enough about the type of person he was that I already sensed I could trust him.

When I was back up to pitch, I decided to throw a curveball.

The batter swung. *Strike!*

I sent another pitch flying, but in a location the batter wasn't expecting. Strike again!

This Coach Driggers is right, I realized. *He does know what he is talking about.*

Another pitch, another strike.

Now I was on a roll again, thanks to Coach. I mixed up my pitches and locations, leaving the batters constantly guessing what I was going to throw. They kept swinging, but they missed more than they hit. The pitching became easier again. And we won the game. Even so, we just couldn't pull off winning the whole series.

One night at the dinner table not long after we had lost in the World Series, Dad nonchalantly asked, "Jon, what would you think about having some private pitching lessons?" Private pitching lessons were not available in Brenham, or if they were, I had not heard of them.

"Like one-on-one lessons?" I asked, trying not to appear overly excited. I had gone to baseball camps where we practiced baseball, but one-on-one coaching was something new—and something I desperately wanted.

He nodded.

"Yeah! I would love that!"

Mom and Dad exchanged a knowing look and then Dad announced, "I spoke with the new baseball coach over at the high school, Coach Driggers. We talked about you and your talent—and he's agreed to work with you privately."

I blinked hard and choked down the food in my mouth. The guy who had been drafted as a pro pitcher was going to work with me? "Wow, Dad! That's great!"

The next week, through the kitchen window, I watched Coach Driggers drive up to the back of our house and get out of his car. He was short and stocky, had a dark tan, and his dark hair was hidden under a green ball cap with a puffy embroidered letter *B* on the front. He wore a white T-shirt that had the Brenham baseball logo in green lettering on the front, elastic gray coaching shorts, calf-high white socks with green stripes, and white turf coaching shoes. He was the real deal.

I grabbed my glove and a few balls and headed outside to meet him. This day had been all I could think about from the moment Dad told me I was getting lessons.

"Jon?" he said and smiled as he closed the car door. "I'm Coach Driggers."

I extended my right hand to shake his hand and looked directly into his eyes.

"It is nice to meet you," he said.

We walked to the backyard and played catch for a while to warm-up. Once I was loose, he asked me to throw some balls so he could observe my style, then he could begin offering suggestions on how to make my pitching even more controlled and powerful. His demeanor was confident as he shared pointers and tidbits on how I could get better. He not only talked about the mechanics of pitching but offered little mental strategies I could implement.

We talked about what pitches to throw during particular counts. For example, with an 0-2 count, he encouraged me to throw a curveball in the dirt or a fastball up and in or a fastball a few inches off the plate. We talked about where hitters would stand. If they were crowding the plate, I should throw the ball inside and vice versa. If the hitter fouled a ball to the opposite side, I should stay with a fastball so the hitter could not allow his bat speed to catch up. If a hitter pulled a ball foul, I needed to think about throwing a changeup on the outer part of the plate.

"Don't be afraid to throw inside and try to work ahead in the count by throwing that first pitch for a strike," he told me.

He encouraged me to use different grips on the ball for different pitches and to continue to see what worked for me. "Throw the curveball out in front of you and let your arm bring your body forward," he said. "Throw through the mitt" and "Make sure you get good balance before going to the plate."

With each piece of advice, he would take the ball from me and say, "Try it like this."

For the curveball, he showed me the grip and threw the ball in a way that made it curve slightly.

I was in awe as I watched him. He was the first person who helped me visualize what I needed to do. For me, talking about it was one thing, but seeing and actually doing it was another.

"Now you try it," he said, flipping the ball back to me.

I gripped the ball just as he had shown me, wound up, and threw. The ball took a slight curve just as Coach's had done.

Every piece of advice he showed me proved to be right each time. It was like instant success.

This guy really *knows what he's talking about*, I thought over and over. I felt better with every pitch and he helped me understand what to do and why it was important to throw in a certain way—such as putting my whole body, rather than just my arm, into the pitch, since doing that could throw out my shoulder or elbow and mess everything up.

The more time I spent with Coach Driggers, the more I respected him. There was something about his demeanor that demanded respect. He was a no-nonsense, type-A personality. For some reason, he took a liking to me too. When a guy like that wanted to help me, I knew he was in my camp and had my best interests at heart, so it was easy for me to do whatever he told me to do. And everything within me wanted to please him. He became my mentor, my hero.

For the next three to four weeks, he coached me two times a week. We always started with the same warm-up, reviewed the previous sessions, and then he instructed me based on what he saw as I pitched. He worked me hard, but I loved every second of it. And when he praised my performance, I was ready to work even harder for him.

After about the second lesson, Dad again raised the topic of baseball during our evening meal together. "Things going well with you and Coach Driggers?"

I nodded, my mouth full of chicken fried steak.

"Do you think it would be more helpful to you if you were able to pitch from an actual mound?"

"Definitely!"

With a "real" mound, Coach Driggers can help me even more, I thought. He'll be able to do wonders with me.

Dad simply nodded. I just figured maybe Coach and I would meet at one of the baseball fields in town to start practicing. That would be pretty cool. I could pretend to be pitching in a "real" game to "real" hitters, I imagined.

After supper, I finished my homework and turned on the television. Dad was sitting at the kitchen table, adjacent and open to the living room where I was, grading tests he had recently given to his college class. He pulled his reading glasses off and laid his red felt pen on top of the stack of graded tests. "Let's see about getting you a mound," he told me.

I couldn't quite compute what he was saying. "What do you mean?"

"Your mother and I think it's time to build a mound for you at the house."

"Like right in the backyard?"

"Yep! Right in the backyard," he said.

Whatever amount of sleepiness I was feeling was instantly replaced with an abundant amount of ecstatic energy. I thought I was going to pass out. Smiling from ear to ear, I thought, *My dream of playing baseball forever is coming true! I love this game! I just love this game!*

The next day, Dad called the local concrete company, Jimmie Hahn, Inc., to inquire about the availability of dirt. This company not only provided concrete but also sold dirt—and not just any dirt. They could get their hands on the good stuff like Texas A&M University used on their baseball field, a high clay-content soil that provided solid footing and would not sink in.

Our good fortune—they had an ample amount in their local yard. Dad ordered what we would need, they delivered it the next day, and over the weekend, we constructed the best and most beautiful mound around.

We measured the size and height so it would be regulation size, just like in professional baseball. It had to be eighteen feet in diameter and ten inches in height. Then we took the dirt and began carefully filling in the area, holding it up with a special clay to keep it intact.

I diligently took care of it daily by lightly watering and raking the dirt and filling in and tamping the holes. When I had it just like I wanted, I covered it with a tarp to prevent any rain from getting on it. I spent hours perfecting my pitching mound. As I worked on that mound every day, my imagination ran wild with dreams of playing baseball forever.

When Coach came for the next lesson, I carefully removed the tarp—Coach was impressed—and took my position at the top. The dirt was compact and solid so I would not slip. I loved that mound, and I loved how my pitching improved as Coach began teaching me from that position.

When Coach arrived and we started the lessons, I felt almost like we were going to church. Whatever he said was gospel to me. I believed every piece of advice, every word, and I always tried to make the changes he recommended. His coaching proved effective—my pitching was getting better each and every time.

Eventually the new school year started and I had to divide my attention between baseball and school work. I was good in school, but I did not particularly like it. To me, school was just something you had to suffer through until you could get back to playing sports. I kept myself busy with playing basketball, something I was also good at, but I did not have the passion for that as I did for baseball. And throughout the year I continued to practice from my pitcher's mound at home. One great thing about living so far south in the United States is that I could play outside all year long.

As baseball season neared, Coach Driggers presented me with a proposal. "I want you to join the high school baseball team as manager for the upcoming season," he told me. "We can talk about the details later, but I want you to consider it."

Consider it? Was he kidding? Of course I would accept that role! How could I turn it down? I mean, after all, that was what I always wanted to do—play baseball. And this way I could be around baseball all the time. Plus, I could learn from the players and, of course, from Coach. He would let me pitch to the hitters, and he would take me to the bull pen with a catcher and work with me.

Without pausing, I shouted out, "Yes!"

He chuckled at my enthusiasm, and told me that I would need to be at every practice and I'd have to arrive early and stay late to help set up and put things away. I would run errands and I would work hard. But I'd also have the opportunity to play some during practices and get extra pitching and batting help. I was all in. *Sign me up!*

"We also need to establish a few requirements before you start," he said.

"What's that?"

"You need to continue to make good grades."

Check that one off the list, I thought. *That's easy.*

"You have to behave in class."

Uhhh, well . . . that might be a little more difficult. I was the class clown—everybody loved to see what crazy stunt I would pull next. But I'd have to curb that one. *Okay, check.*

"And I would like to see you lose some weight so you're more agile, especially for pitching. The better shape you are in, the better your performance."

Yeah, I want to, but that's a tough one. I'm not sure how to do that.

As if reading my mind, he said, "I'll help you. We will start with a simple running program. You'll also need to limit how much you are eating."

Gulp. *Okay, check.*

Coach had never led me astray, so I would do what he asked. And if I kept my focus on the fact that I would get to play more baseball, the other stuff was not so hard to handle.

Game on! "Okay, Coach, I will. I'll do those things," I told him. I worked hard to fulfill my commitment and was determined not to fail. He made a deal with me, and it was time to honor my part.

I kept my grades up. That was the easiest of the requirements.

I started running and watching what I ate, and as the weight started to fall off, I felt better about myself both mentally and physically. I began to run more and more and actually started to enjoy it. Oddly enough, you would think I exercised a lot, just because my mom was a physical education teacher, but when she encouraged me to exercise, I never wanted to because I felt like she was nagging me. But when Coach encouraged me to exercise, I felt different—not that he was nagging me but that he wanted me to be the best player I could be, which meant being healthier and in better physical shape. That requirement was not so bad either.

My behavior, though? It was off and on. My problem was that if someone dared me to do something, I would do it. Didn't matter what it was. I just loved that feeling of acceptance when people laughed at my antics. I often overheard others comment how I was a crazy kid. They'd say that I beat to a different drum. But the truth is, they did not really know me. I acted up and caused scenes because I felt so fearful of being rejected and desperately wanted people's approval. Because I was so afraid I would not get it, I became childish and volatile. It's the never-ending cycle that goes nowhere. I was trying to get others' attention, not knowing what else to do and not doing it all that well. I felt so odd and fat that if I could make people laugh, then I was somebody.

I was the kid who lit firecrackers at school to make kids scream and go crazy. I was the kid who hung underwear on the flagpole to see the reaction of the principal, or who took a semester exam from the teacher's desk a few days before the testing.

Life without some sort of drama was not interesting. I loved the thrill of keeping others in suspense—the suspense of what kind of trick I was going to pull next. I loved to surprise others, causing them to laugh or catching them off guard in total disbelief.

I was also enthralled with the thrill of getting caught—or not getting caught. Perhaps that is why I tried such outlandish things.

Punishment did not come my way much. It must have been the way I smiled at just the right time or the gentle tone of my words. When I found myself in trouble, I was usually in for a good talking-to, but that was it. I guess they thought that would change my behavior, but in reality, I was searching for so much more. I just wanted to be treated like all the other kids but for some reason, I never felt that way. So I tried hard to behave, just as Coach asked me to, but from time to time, I would still act up. I just never created any major problems and there were never any consequences.

Until one dreadful day about a month into my stint as the high school baseball manager.

"Hey, Jon," one of my classmates whispered to me before our math class started. "I dare you to put a tack on Mrs.

Flasowski's chair." Our teacher had not yet entered the classroom, so this would be the easiest dare ever. My friend raised his eyebrows, as if to say, *Well? What are you waiting for?*

Kids do stupid things. It's like their thought process is delayed and distorted by what they think for a split second will be the funny or cool thing to do. They impulsively act out, not realizing that their decisions may not be the smartest. And at this particular moment, I was one of those stupid kids.

I put my hand out to accept the tack he had ready and waiting for me. And in the commotion of people entering the classroom and getting settled, I quickly headed to Mrs. Flasowski's desk, nonchalantly stepped behind it, as though I were looking for something on her desk, placed the tack squarely in the middle of her chair, and then casually walked back to my seat, wearing a wide smile and watching my friend's face light up with mischievous delight.

The bell rang and in walked Mrs. Flasowski. "Good morning, class," she said and began discussing what we were going to cover in that day's lesson. Back and forth she paced, as I waited for her to move to her seat. Finally, with a break in her lecture and putting us to work completing our math assignment, she headed to her chair. My friends and I watched intently to see her reaction. We were all snickering and trying to hold it in.

It was too late. She sat and immediately bounced back up with a squeaky scream. It was not as funny as I had thought it would be. She really looked hurt, and I felt terrible that I had done that.

"*Jon!*"

Busted!

Her face turned bright red and she pointed toward the door. "Go to the principal's office. Right now!"

My friends were still chuckling, and to save face, I smiled and made it seem like it was no big deal—that I had pulled off the prank of the century. But inside, I felt regret for what I had done to her. She was not a bad person, but I had treated her with disrespect—just to be accepted by my friends.

I was good at negotiating my way out of situations. Usually I would get to the principal's office and he would ask, "What are you here for?" I'd shrug and act innocent and say, "I don't know." Most of the time it worked and he would tell me to knock it off and then send me back to class.

This time I entered the principal's office and he said, "What are you here for now?"

I shrugged and acted innocent. "I don't know. Mrs. Flasowski told me to come down here."

"What do you mean you don't know?"

"I don't know. Something happened when she sat down, and she got up and told me to come to the principal's office."

He furled his eyebrows and grabbed his phone. After a few quick sentences with the person on the other line, he hung up. "Did you put a tack on Mrs. Flasowski's chair?"

"I don't know what you're talking about." I was certain he'd tell me to knock it off and I would get off and go back to class.

This was not one of those times.

"What am I going to do with you, Mr. Peters?" the principal said to me.

I sighed inwardly and thought, *I'm probably going to get paddled.* I had received licks with wooden paddles in the past (when schools were still allowed to spank kids) and those had failed to change my behavior. Hard, forceful swats on the backside did not transmit to my brain. I just thought the whole thing was more annoying.

"For the rest of this week, during lunch period, you're going to help the cafeteria ladies out."

"What's that mean?"

"You're going to get a broom and you're going to sweep the floor," he said. "Perhaps a more humiliating approach to your discipline will bring some change in you."

That's not so bad, I thought. I figured I would be the center of attention and everyone would laugh at what I had done and think it was cool.

"You can go back to class now," he said dismissively.

So for the next three days, as my instigators ate, I swept. They watched me and laughed. I hated every minute as I pushed that four-foot broom all around the cafeteria. They did not think it was cool. And I was the center of attention, but as a joke.

One of those days while I was sweeping, Coach's wife, Sharon, who just so happened to teach at my school, was in the cafeteria. She watched me maneuver my way between rows of tables and chairs. With a smile, she asked me what I was doing.

I smiled back and in a heartfelt and soft tone replied, "Oh, Mrs. Driggers, I'm just helping out the cafeteria ladies. One less chore they have to do."

After school, I grabbed my book bag and headed out to the parking lot. The trainer picked me up and took me across town to the baseball stadium where the high school held their practices and games. Since I was only in eighth grade and not old enough to drive, Coach made sure that the trainer got me to and from school and the stadium.

We changed into our baseball uniforms in the parking lot behind the first base dugout—something we did for both games and practices. There were no locker rooms, so we shielded our bodies from public view with players' cars and trucks. It became a baseball tradition for us.

After getting dressed, I walked into the stadium to help set up the field and saw Coach standing at the entrance. Instead of his usual nod (his way of saying hello), he stared me down.

"Tack in a teacher's seat, huh?"

I was not prepared to hear that. He had caught me completely off guard. Apparently, his wife had found out the truth and told him what I had done.

In our small town, word spread like wildfire. And most of the time, the word was true. It was hard to keep anything from anybody. It was like there was a central speaker in town and every day, we were updated about who was doing what, when, and where.

A rush of panic came over me. My heart began to pound, while rage started brewing inside me. My face turned red and my body temperature began heating up as though I was preparing for a fight with a fierce competitor—a fight that, if I was not prepared, I stood no chance of winning.

Previously, I had always reverted back to my norm—either fighting with all my might or running away as fast and as far as my legs endured. I would use words of hatred and cursing in order to defend my position and tear my accuser down. It was my usual defense and the only way I knew of protecting myself. But that day, rational thought settled over my mind. I knew if I reverted back, I would lose everything I had worked so hard for. And I would disappoint Coach. He had given me this great opportunity to be part of the team. And if I messed it up by allowing my temper to get the best of me, it would all be over. So I took a different approach, one I had never taken before.

After what seemed like an eternity but I'm sure was only a matter of seconds, I looked directly at Coach and replied, "Yes, sir. That was me." For the first time, I admitted what I had done instead of attempting to weasel my way out of it. It actually felt good, freeing, but it was also scary.

"After practice, you owe us some conditioning," was all he said.

I knew exactly what that meant. Conditioning was a dreaded part of every practice. Although I was in good shape and ran all the time with no problems, butterflies still churned inside my stomach at the thought of running. It was that uneasy feeling of anxious and nervous energy.

After practice, I stayed. And Coach had me run from one foul pole to the other—back and forth, foul pole to foul pole in a minute. I ran and ran and ran. Then I had to do pickups, where he threw a ball to the right of me, and I shuffled to get it. And then he threw one to my left. Back and forth I shuffled over and over. I was exhausted. My legs were numb with a tingling sensation, and were weak and heavy, as though I was dragging around a ton of bricks with each step.

But I deserved every moment of it. This was the first time I was ever really disciplined and the first time I accepted my part. It hurt; it was torturous. But I accepted it, because I knew what I had done was wrong. Coach Driggers was not just teaching me about baseball, he was teaching me about life. And I had a lot of learning still to do.

CHAPTER 7

THE CHURCH OF BASEBALL, A GOOD BUDDY, AND A BEAUTIFUL GIRLFRIEND

I was feeling good. I had lost a lot of weight, was in the best shape of my life, and had learned my lesson enough that for all the fun-loving attention I yearned for, I longed even more for my coach's approval. I did *not* want to disappoint Coach Driggers again, so I did my best to keep on his good side.

He noticed. And when I became a freshman and moved up to high school, where he became my official coach, he placed me on the varsity team—rare for a freshman. He continued to spend time with me, encouraging and challenging me always to be in better shape physically and mentally. He worked hard to get me into spiritual shape as well. A Christian, Coach Driggers did not shy away from talking about God. He didn't beat it down our throats, but he would talk about his faith in bits and pieces in front of the players. After every practice and before and after every game, we said the Lord's Prayer. He'd also give us coaching talks each day. I liked that he never just said, "Hey, team, how are you doing? Let's go out there and do a great job." He was always about teaching us to be better—both on the field and off. He would talk about the three *D*s—dedication, discipline, and devotion. Some of the players didn't like his methods—they just wanted to play ball. I wanted to play ball too, but there was something about the way he talked and his strict expectations that I liked. He was tough—but I felt as though he genuinely cared about me as a person.

Even so, I wasn't all that interested in the God stuff. I went to church, so I figured that was good enough. Besides, I did not need God. I was doing fine on my own. I still struggled with the insecurities, but I didn't consider that maybe God could help me with those. I thought it was just something I had to deal with on my own. And when I played baseball, those insecurities disappeared, so I figured I would just continue to play ball!

After all, our high school varsity team was doing well, and we were ranked number one in the state. We had solid players, and the upperclassmen treated me with respect, even though I was just a freshman—although most of them already knew me from my time the previous year as the team manager. I even made a new best friend, who was just as passionate about baseball as I was.

Jeff Toll was our team manager. He was a sophomore I knew in passing (since in a small town everybody knows everybody). He had played Little League on teams I sometimes competed against, but I didn't really get to know him until this season started. He had always been a short, scrawny kid, and he wasn't strong enough to play baseball, but he loved it as much as he loved breathing. Just to be around the game and players seemed to be good enough for him.

He and I would sit together for hours and rub the new baseballs to make sure they weren't too slick for pitching. The whole time we were grinding the leather, we would talk baseball—players, teams, stats, highlights, favorite games.

"You love this game so much," I told him one day, "why haven't you tried out to actually play it? You played in Little League, I remember."

He shook his head and smiled sadly. "Can't," he said. "I've got leukemia."

I stopped gripping the baseball and looked at him. "Oh, man, I'm sorry. I didn't know." I guess I should have known, because of all that small town knowing everybody and everything, but for some reason, it had never registered with me.

He shrugged, as if to say, *It is what it is.*

"Are you okay?"

"Yeah," he said. "It comes and goes. I got it when I was fourteen. I had to go to the hospital and have a bunch of tests done." He shrugged again. "You know, I wouldn't be surprised if our team makes it all the way to state this year."

"Hope so." I think we were both relieved to change the subject, but his news stuck with me. I'd had no idea he was ill. I wasn't sure exactly what leukemia was, but I knew it wasn't good. I was struck by the fact that he lived with it every day but never seemed to allow it to control his attitude. I wondered how he did that.

I complained and moaned when the smallest, most insignificant things didn't go my way, and next to Jeff, I had nothing to complain about! I found myself wanting to spend more time with Jeff to see how he managed life. Not just because of his attitude toward his disease, but also because, just as I knew Coach Driggers believed in me, I knew Jeff did too. There was something special about him—he could make you feel as though you were the most important person in the world, that he genuinely cared about you. I wanted what he had to rub off on me! I liked who I was when I was around him. What I didn't realize was that special quality about him was his faith. Unlike Coach Driggers, Jeff didn't talk much about God. He quietly lived a life of faith, showing Jesus' love and compassion to others. Sometimes he might say something about church or his youth group, but just as I did with Coach Driggers's faith, I didn't think a contented life had anything to do with God.

For me the God stuff was what I did on Sundays because my mother insisted on it. Going to church was just something we did, along with being forced to follow a bunch of rules. In baseball I found freedom, not in God.

So while I loved Coach Driggers and my friend Jeff, I believed their faith worked for them, and that was great. But it was not something for me.

I continued to worship at the church of baseball. And my work showed my faithfulness and loyalty. I was ready for my first varsity playoffs. Another step toward my goals. College coaches look at high school teams, and I was a freshman playing varsity. I knew I was sure to get attention. But I was surprised by how much attention!

One afternoon after practice as we were getting ready to start the playoffs, Coach Driggers called us into a huddle.

"Guys, I've decided we're going to go one game throughout the playoffs," he said.

In Texas at that time, a playoff series was the best-of-three games, but if one coach wanted to play a one-game playoff, then the teams would play only one game. Sort of a winner takes it all.

I sighed inwardly. *There goes my chance to prove myself in the playoffs*, I thought, then I looked at our other pitcher, David Crowson. He was a senior. (Later, he got drafted by the Mets.) I breathed in deeply and waited to hear Coach announce David's name.

"And I'm going with Peters as the pitcher."

I blinked hard. He said my name. *Oh my,* I thought. *He really does believe in me.*

I found Jeff in the huddle. He was smiling from ear to ear. Then I glanced toward David, sure he would be upset. But he just smiled too.

My knees felt wobbly. One game. Do or die. If we lost this game, we lost the series. If we lost the series, we lost our shot at the state championship. One game. And it lay squarely on my shoulders.

"You can do this," Jeff told me as practice ended. "You're really good. You'll win it, for sure."

I nodded. I knew I could do it, but I also had that twinge of fear and panic. What if I couldn't? What if I failed? What if the team all hated me because I didn't succeed?

The condemning thoughts came over me, pounding me as a thunderstorm pummels the earth. This religion was all I knew. My faith in the game couldn't let me down.

And it didn't. We breezed right through the playoffs, beating most of our opponents by ten runs or more. My confidence was soaring. Even though my thoughts before each game were doom and gloom—*I might get beat this game. They might hit me hard tonight. I hope I have my good stuff*—as soon as I threw that first pitch, my nerves calmed and it was "game on!" *Sit down, boy! You can't hit this!* It was as if a switch had been turned on and my competitive nature was in full force. I became cocky, arrogant, and bulldoggish.

During one game my nerves got the better of me. Our team was headed to the state tournament and we were to play the Snyder Tigers in the semifinal game. The week prior to the tournament, I read up on the team. All the newspaper articles wrote about our matchup and they referenced how Snyder was hitting close to .400 as a team and how they had dominated teams with their bats.

Wow, these guys must be able to hit. This is going to be a tough game!

I started brooding over the idea that I might not be able to pitch well enough against them. We had one game to win it, and if I had an off night, we were done.

My nerves, which usually went away after the first pitch of the game, felt wild and out of control, and that game's first pitch—a fastball—got away from me. I hit the right-handed leadoff batter in the ribs. It didn't glance off him; it hit him squarely in the ribs, stuck in his gut for a second, and then dropped straight to the ground. My arm went numb and I couldn't feel any part of my body. I had to tell myself which body part to move, and when it did, it felt like I was in slow motion. But after that pitch, I settled down, and we beat Snyder 10-0 in five innings.

After the game, my dad told me that our catcher's dad, Jack Fisher, confessed to him: "That's probably the best thing Jon could have done. Now the Snyder boys won't dig in and get so comfortable."

We took state that year (and David got to pitch the State Championship game). By the end of the season, I had an ERA of 1.97, which meant I allowed around two earned runs per game. I pitched eighty-five and a third innings, and I finished the season with a 13-0 record (thirteen wins, zero losses) with ninety-four strikeouts and nineteen walks.

As if that weren't enough, my All-Star team had once again gone a long way that summer, this time to the Senior Little League World Series. We finished second in the world. We lost to Taipei, Taiwan—the team known for winning many Little League World Series' titles. We held our own and competed well, and we proudly held our heads high as the United States' champions.

The baseball gods had come through for me again.

• • •

I slid into my sophomore year on a cloud. I was the sensational pitcher for our beloved Brenham High Cubs. Everywhere in town I went, I would hear somebody yell out my name.

"Atta boy, Peters! Make us proud."

"You're doing a great job, Jon!"

"You're set for the major leagues for sure."

And I believed it. Everything was going my way. I pitched the best I had ever pitched all through my sophomore year—it was as though I *couldn't* fail. My pitches were consistently in the eighty-nine to ninety-two miles per hour range. My coach and mentor believed in me. My friend Jeff was a constant source of encouragement. And I had Jill.

Jill was a freshman. With blonde hair, olive-complexioned skin, a tall athletic body, and a smile that could melt me in an instant, Jill was beautiful.

For some reason, I had never noticed her at school. But one weekend, while my friend Steven Gurka and I were driving around town, we pulled into the cinema parking lot and she was standing in line with a senior from our school.

Wow! I thought and immediately asked Steven, "Who is that?"

He told me, and I wondered how he knew and I didn't! What had I been missing?

The following Monday, I had Coach Driggers for Health, and I sat next to Amber Dannhaus, who was a freshman.

"Hey, Amber," I asked before class started. "Do you know Jill?"

"Yeah. Why?"

I felt my throat constrict. I shrugged. "Just wondering." I was too embarrassed and shy to admit I was interested in Jill. I was not the baseball star; I was the fat kid who couldn't button his uniform pants.

She'd never be interested in me, I thought.

The next day in class, Amber smiled and leaned across the aisle. "I told Jill you asked about her. She seemed very interested."

My heart sped up and my palms got sweaty. This was exactly what I wanted—and what I didn't want. I felt much better *wanting* to know her and not being rejected than meeting her and having all my fears realized. *She's going to hate me*, I told myself.

I nodded to Amber, trying to play it cool. But inside, I started to count the minutes until I could get home, find out her phone number, and call her for a date.

She agreed, which stunned and excited me, and we settled on that next weekend. Friday night I picked her up from her house in my teal green Cutlass Supreme and drove us to Tejas, a local restaurant in Brenham, and then we went to a movie.

Just being near her, I felt so proud, like *I'm the man!*

After that night, we quickly started dating each other exclusively.

Jill was kind and wonderful and beautiful. And she liked me. I had it all: baseball, a good friend, and a gorgeous girlfriend. What could go wrong?

CHAPTER 8

TROUBLE BEGINS

"Jon, you got a minute? I'd like to talk with you," Coach said one day after we had finished practice.

"Sure, Coach." I dropped my bag and followed him to the first base dugout.

He sat on the bench and motioned for me to sit to his left. I was sure he wanted to strategize with me over the upcoming playoffs.

"Jon, I've got some good news for you. I've nominated you to try out for the US team at this year's Junior Olympics. Usually the players are seniors, but I was able to convince them to give you an exemption because of your talent."

"Wow, that's great!" I couldn't believe it. I was headed to the Junior Olympics!

"The tryouts are in North Carolina this summer, so you'll go there for several weeks before the Olympics begin."

"Okay, that sounds good. Thank you, Coach. This means a lot." I couldn't wait to tell Jill, Jeff, and my parents. Everybody would be excited for me.

I started to get up from the bench when Coach interrupted me. "There's something else."

Something else? I wondered. *What could be better than being on the US Junior Olympics team?*

"I've received an offer to be the head coach at Tarleton State University. I start with them this fall." He paused. I guess he was waiting for me to let his news soak in.

His words were not making sense. He told me I had made tryouts for the United States Junior Olympic team, and then he said something about taking another coaching job. Then with a tsunami force, his words hit. He was leaving Brenham High School. He was leaving . . . me.

He's leaving? Now? A million thoughts rushed through my mind, all banging into one another, and causing the rest of my body to feel nauseated and weak.

But I need him. He's my coach, now *what am I going to do? Why does he have to go now?*

A darkness fell over me and I felt lost. Alone.

Finally, when I didn't say anything, he continued. "I wanted to tell you in person, rather than have you find out with the rest of the team or from somebody else."

Still no words came, but at least I managed a nod. Really, all I wanted to do was cry and beg him not to go.

"Coach Hathaway will be your head coach next year," he said. Coach Hathaway was the assistant and was a very good collegiate ball player, so my head told me we were in good hands. But my heart still ached.

I nodded again.

"Hey, Jon, I'm just one call away."

I knew he meant it, but still I walked out of the dugout as though in a trance. I no longer cared about the Junior Olympics. I just wanted my coach back.

• • •

It was the summer of 1987. Our high school team had just won its second consecutive state baseball title. (Coach Driggers did the same thing with the playoff series as he did when I was a freshman—making it a one-game series and having me pitch.) And my record for the season was 15-0 (fifteen wins, zero losses).

No one understood how desperately afraid and lost I felt. Coach Driggers was the man who had taken an excited, talented, insecure, young kid and turned him into a pitching force. I did the work, but Coach was the one who saw how I could be better and then expected me to follow through. Coach never let me slide on anything. Now he was gone and I felt achingly, painfully alone.

"That's a shame, but Coach Hathaway is good. You'll do well with him," people would say. "And now you're going to the Junior Olympic trials!"

As the days approached for me to travel to North Carolina, I became more and more excited and nervous. I had never been away from my family and friends for an extended period of time. Though my parents would be driving out, they would not arrive for at least a week. And Coach Driggers had already moved on.

I flew into the Raleigh-Durham International Airport, got a shuttle to the University of North Carolina, and registered with all the others who were selected to try out. They were all older than me and seemed more at ease, more assured of themselves. I strangely desired to get back on a plane and fly home. I knew I was good—but all those insecurities came rushing back. Sure, I was good against other ball players in my region, but these were the best of the best from all over the country. What if I failed? What if I couldn't measure up? What if I let down Coach Driggers?

I reminded myself that Coach believed in me and thought I was good enough to stand up with any of these other guys, so I sucked in my anxieties and tried to act like I belonged there just as much as everybody else.

I was relieved to meet my assigned suitemate for the time I'd be there. Steve Medina was an outfielder from Beeville, in south Texas, who had recently graduated and signed a scholarship with Texas A&M University. He was one of my people—a Texas boy! He and I connected right away because we knew all the same places. He helped relieve some of the terror of meeting so many new people, not a strong suit of mine.

The first few days were scheduled practices to prepare for the upcoming games. The coaches divided all of us into four separate teams from all parts of the country. At the end of the competition, the best would be selected for the United States' team to play in Cuba.

At sixteen years old, I was the youngest, having just completed my sophomore year of high school. The other players, most of whom were eighteen and nineteen, were mature and more seasoned. As they boasted about their accomplishments, their confidence rang out with cockiness and arrogance as loud as a firehouse bell. They walked with a bounce in their step, their chests bowed out, and their chins stuck out high. Most were not afraid to ridicule their opponents with sarcastic words that sounded like degrading, pent-up hate, laughing and carrying on as long as people listened.

I knew I could come off sometimes as cocky, but I was a naïve, small-town boy, who wasn't used to this level of pride or confidence. Although I knew I had talent and determination, I preferred to stay in the background and watch. *Don't get too showy or they'll start talking smack about me next*, I realized. The longer I was there, those insecurities came back out. I was way out of my league. I'd watch the guys throw and think, *They are so much better than me! They're going to show me up.* I knew I was good and could consistently throw ninety-mile-an-hour balls, but I never felt like I was good *enough*. I felt scared of failing.

I don't fit in here. No way am I going to make this team, I thought. *I'm going to fail. I am going to let everybody down. They're going to laugh at me.*

Once I was on the field I still felt at ease. I knew I could prove my worth and abilities there. But when I was alone, lying in bed at night, or listening to the smack talk of the others, those defeating thoughts consumed me.

The pitching practices consisted of throwing balls in the morning and then again in the afternoon. We were throwing nonstop, and I noticed my arm started to feel sore. I never mentioned that to any of the coaches, though, because nobody else was complaining, and I didn't want anyone to think I was being a whiner.

After almost a week of practice, we were ready to start the tryout games. Even with a sore arm, I had performed well during the practices. If history had anything to say about it, my dominance on the mound was to take place very soon. I was a "gamer"; I thrived in competition and, when challenged, I rose to the top of my game. Others could not beat me mentally, regardless of what antics they pulled. And physically, if they did beat me, then they earned it, because I was not giving it up easily.

First impressions can have a lasting impact. Professional scouts lined the fences with stopwatches, radar guns, and player cards in hand. Fans from all across the United States filled the stadium with cameras and scorecards. Parents sat together in their section with hopes their sons performed well. And I was aware of it all.

The day of our first tryout game had arrived. I walked to the front of the dugout and looked at the lineup card posted on the wall with white athletic training tape. There it was, written boldly with a black Sharpie pen: RELIEF PITCHER—JON PETERS. I took in a deep breath. It was time to shine and get my game on. This was my chance.

I was scheduled to pitch a few designated innings of relief work. That was perfect with me because it allowed me ample time to get ready, both physically and mentally. And when my body and mind were in sync, I was tough to beat. I wanted to destroy and eliminate the opponent. I wanted it to be clear that *I* was the champion. I may not keep up with these guys off the field, but I knew once I was in the "zone," I could hold my own very well.

The game started and I sat in the dugout watching and cheering for my team. But my mind wouldn't focus on the game. I felt out of sync. The self-condemning thoughts kept bombarding me, but something else was wrong too. As much as I tried to settle my inner demons, I just couldn't. My gut hinted at something in disarray, but *what* remained a mystery.

"Peters!" The pitching coach called out. "Head over to the bull pen and start warming up."

I nodded, forced my thoughts to silence, and headed out.

From my first step out of the third base dugout to my jog down left field, I could feel everyone's eyes on me. The new kid was getting warmed up. But instead of feeling excitement from them, I imagined they all knew something was wrong, that I was going to mess up.

I stepped into the bull pen and nodded toward my catcher, then I got into my position, and gripped the ball. I always used my warm-up routine as a time to prepare my mind and body to engage. It was the start of the competition, determining success or failure, and was the most important part of my performance. It was like my "happy place" where I tuned out all distractions and became perfectly in sync with my mission.

My happy place was not so happy this time around, though. I threw the first pitch and felt something tingle in my shoulder. I moved my shoulder and arm around, thinking they were just cold and needed a little more loosening. But the next pitch brought more tingling and pain.

Arm pain and soreness were not uncommon for me. Every pitcher who consistently throws ninety-mile-an-hour balls over and over will have some sort of ache. That's why during games, pitchers will have their arms and shoulders covered with jackets and heating packs. They're doing everything they can to keep their arms limber and the ache away. My pain typically never came before or during a game, though. I experienced it more the day after a game, and then it quickly disappeared after a proper warm-up. But on this night—a time to showcase my talent in front of thousands of key, influential baseball personnel—the discomfort was not lessening. With every throw and stretch, my shoulder grew tenser, as though someone were squeezing my nerve and slowly twisting. I tried stretching and then throwing, but nothing would help. After each release and follow-through with the ball, the strings of ligaments and tendons felt so tightly wound, it seemed with the wrong movement, they would quickly turn into pieces of frayed yarn.

I could not force the pain to stop, no matter what I did. My mind became obsessed with this feeling of abnormality. *Come on, Jon*, I told myself. *Get it together. Come on. Come on! This isn't good. I don't need this. Not right now. I can't fail. This is my one shot!*

The stiffness of my body coupled with the pressure I placed on myself to dominate and make a positive, lasting impression was not helping. Every surefire trick I tried seemed to cause more harm than good. The tingling had turned to zapping, as though an electric prod was searing into my shoulder. But I was not giving up. *It's just jitters*, I told myself. *Just get out there and get in the zone, then it will all be okay. I'll be fine.*

The inning was over. "Peters, you're up," the pitching coach yelled.

I inhaled deeply. I had done the preparation, now there was nothing else to do but go out there and compete.

Once I'm on the mound, the pain will go away, I thought. *It's just nerves. I'm always nervous before I pitch, and this is a huge game, that's why I'm feeling so tense.* I could not blow this opportunity. This was my shot to make it big. This is exactly what I had dreamed about since I was six years old. *Pitch well and write your own ticket. Anything else and your chances are flushed down the toilet. You can do this!*

I jogged briskly from the bull pen to the mound. A good run usually got my juices flowing. The umpire met me at the mound and tossed me a brand-new pearl—a baseball. I proceeded to go through my normal mound ritual of smoothing the areas of raised dirt and rubbing the gloss off the ball. It was the little things that mattered. Attention to the details led to my competitive advantage.

The pulsing sensation radiating from my shoulder and down through my fingertips was still there as I threw the warm-up pitches. *If I can get through the two innings I'm scheduled to pitch, I can figure it out later*, I told myself. I had no other option than to suck it up and pitch my best game ever. Losers allowed pain to get to them, using it as an excuse. Winners endured pain to achieve the goal. Whatever it took, I was going to be a winner.

The pain's intensity escalated with each pitch. I had never experienced this feeling before. The throbbing, tingling sensation fell in sync with my every heartbeat. Something was not right. And by the look of others' facial expressions, they knew it too.

I took the ball again, determined to push through the pain. As I wound up and released the ball toward the catcher, my arm felt as though it snapped off and went with the throw. Intense, searing pain shot through my shoulder and traveled down my arm to my fingers. It felt as though a bomb had exploded inside my body.

The next thing I knew I was lying on the ground surrounded by the coaches and some of the players all hovering over me and looking down at me. I don't know how I got in that position or how long I had been there.

"You okay, son?" one of the coaches asked.

No, I'm not. "Yeah, I think so. My arm . . ."

A few guys helped me to my feet and walked me off the field to a waiting ambulance.

At the hospital, the medical staff gave me medicine for the pain and then took me for tests. Some of the Olympics' staff were in the room with me, having followed the ambulance to the hospital. No one said much. We all knew whatever happened was not good.

After what seemed like hours, the doctor came back in my room. "I'm going to give you some medication to decrease the pain. There is nothing life-threatening here so I'm clearing you to fly back to Texas to consult an orthopedic surgeon there. It may just require rest. Let's keep our fingers crossed."

My Junior Olympic days were done.

That night I was back in the dorm, my shoulder harnessed up tightly so I couldn't move it. My parents had just arrived from driving the long distance. Now Dad was turning around to head back to Texas while Mom was flying back with me to go home.

The next day on the plane ride into College Station—forty miles from Brenham—I felt empty, lonely, and relieved. *I'm out because I'm not that good*, I thought, followed quickly by, *I just let Coach down and I let down the whole town of Brenham.*

To make matters worse, when we landed and I was walking off the plane, I caught sight of a bunch of people from Brenham, including Jill, there to greet me. They cheered and waved, as though they were supporting an important somebody. Thick, salty tears welled up in my eyes. *I let them down. I'm just not good enough.*

Everybody was sympathetic and excited for me that I'd even been there for the tryouts, as though it didn't matter that I didn't make it. They just wanted me to be okay and were proud of me, but I could not hear that from them. I just wanted to crawl into my bed at home and lie in the darkness.

The next morning my mother's voice floated into my room. "Jon? I got you an appointment to meet with Dr. Bryan. He's the Astros' team physician."

My parents helped me get ready, since with each movement of my shoulder, a sharp pain radiated down my arm. We drove the hour and an half or so to Houston to Dr. William Bryan's office.

During the entire drive I kept hoping Dr. Bryan would take a look and say everything was okay, that I just needed some rest. But deep down, I feared it was worse than that. I could handle anything, just not losing my ability to play baseball. I might not have felt I fit in with the Junior Olympic players, but I definitely felt more at home playing ball in Brenham.

Doctor Bryan did an arthrogram, in which he stuck a needle into my shoulder joint and injected it with dye, so they could see a greater extent of the problem when they do an MRI.

If I thought the pain of the tear was bad, my shoulder felt on fire when he pushed a needle into that joint. I tried not to cry, but boy, it hurt!

After the test, he came back into his office to share the results. "There is a tear in your anterior capsule. The good news is that we can repair it arthroscopically. It's really not a big deal; we can get this taken care of for you."

Music to my ears.

"So I can play ball this coming season?" I asked, feeling hopeful for the first time since the injury.

"You can play ball this coming season," he assured me.

Whew, this is good. We'll get this fixed and I'll get back out onto the field.

Everyone was excited by the news. This was nothing to worry about, no big deal. And I'd be back and just as good as I ever was.

Only I wasn't.

CHAPTER 9
BREAKING THE RECORD

The surgery was quick and then I started working rehab with direction from the Astros' team trainer to get the shoulder back into shape. The trainer suggested I begin a strength and conditioning program involving lightweight dumbbells, rubber resistance bands, and stretching exercises. The great Astros' pitcher Nolan Ryan had developed this program, and considering he was my childhood hero and I wanted to be just like him, it was easy for me to get motivated to religiously perform the recommended exercises. I became fearless and not a day went by without doing my workout program. I was committed to getting back on top. Others were depending on me and I was not going to let them—or myself—down.

I knew if I didn't get my arm and shoulder back into shape, my dream was over. And I knew everyone was watching me to see if I was really going to come back—a huge expectation for the small town of Brenham! Worse things had happened to others, I reminded myself, yet they had found ways to get back on top again. I was determined to do that too. Giving up on my dream was not an option; it was something losers did, and I had something to prove. I had not finished what I'd started. So I worked hard and followed everything the trainer told me to do. I started to feel good again. Plus I had the fall and winter to rest it before spring came, along with our next season.

My junior year started and we weren't that far into the first semester when one afternoon Coach Hathaway saw me in the hall and stopped me. "Hey, Jon, come by the rubber gym when you get a minute, will you? I want to talk with you." The building was a secondary gym at the high school that had a rubber floor. We had pitching mounds made of wood and covered with Astroturf and an indoor batting cage so we could practice in inclement weather. The gym was used for PE classes, off-season athletics, and basketball practice.

"Okay. I'll hurry over before our off-season period," I told him. After third period, I headed straight to the rubber gym. "Hey, Coach."

"Have a seat." Coach motioned to a chair. I didn't like where this was going. The last time I'd had a conversation like this, Coach Driggers told me he was leaving. But as I looked at Coach Hathaway, he seemed relaxed and excited about something. "I received a call from a reporter who informed me that a potential national record is in the making this coming season."

"Oh, yeah? For what?"

"The most consecutive wins by a high school pitcher. The current record is thirty-three. You're at twenty-eight."

I could break that record?

Coach smiled. "With the amount of talent on our returning team, you have a real shot."

My rehabilitation was progressing as expected. I had no doubt I was coming back as healthy as ever. I was laser focused on staying in tip-top shape. My coaches and teammates didn't have to worry about me putting in the extra work and doing my part to prepare for the upcoming season. I fed off others' energy and off my own focus, never letting up. I believed in the mission—to win a third consecutive state championship. And now I had a national record to consider as well.

"Thanks, Coach." He didn't have to tell me what I already knew. If the national record really was looming within my grasp, I was going to hear about it—and inquiries on my recovery—from a lot more media. I had become familiar with the reporters during the past two seasons. Because of the previous success and reputation of our baseball program, it was common to see reporters periodically throughout the season. I had spoken with many of them and either listened to them on the radio or watched them on television. They were good people and always respectful. The success we had accomplished as a team was attractive, and as it was playing out, I knew we were going to see a lot more of them. If they were already looking forward to the season and had contacted Coach Hathaway about the record, then what was it going to be like when we actually got into the season?

Sure enough, Coach would tell me about some reporter who had contacted him, or I would receive a phone call at home from someone wanting to ask what I thought about the upcoming season, the possible record breaking game, or my recovery.

At times while talking to a reporter I would laugh and think, *You guys must be really bored and desperate for a story to want to talk with me.* Here I was, a seventeen-year-old high school junior who was just a normal kid and not much different from anyone else. I happened to love baseball and I was good at pitching, but there were other kids just like me and even better. If I traveled one hour in each direction, I was surrounded by major universities with elite athletes—or better yet, professional sports teams. But they were choosing to cover a high school pitcher. I did not understand that.

As January rolled around, the excitement began to mount even more. The preseason rankings were released and, once again, we were ranked number one in Class 4A. To us, the rankings were just that—rankings. It did not matter how we started the season; how we *ended* was our focus. On any given day, we matched up well against any team in the state and had the potential to win, even against the bigger schools. Bigger was not always better in the state of Texas. We had proven that over and over again during our non-district schedule.

All around town the talk centered around my winning streak and the Cubs returning to Austin, the city where the state baseball championship took place. Schedules were blocked way in advance, reflecting "out of office" in preparation for our return appearance. And if we returned, the town would almost completely shut down as fans traveled to support the baseball team. The joke around town was, "If you ever wanted to rob a store and not get caught, the time to do it was during a baseball game." With everyone at the park, the city was like a ghost town.

By the first week of February, our whole team was more than ready to begin practicing. I felt ready, strong. But as I began practicing more in earnest, something was different. My shoulder injury had healed—the tests proved it. Maybe subconsciously I was afraid of reinjuring it. I don't know, but I do know that my pitching changed and my throws did not have the same velocity as before. I began to throw more with my arm in a herky-jerky motion than using the whole of my shoulder and body. As hard as I worked, I could never quite reach the ninety-mile-an-hour range. I was consistently now throwing in the eighty-five/eighty-six range.

Without Coach Driggers there to catch my mechanics and help me fix them—even though Coach Hathaway proved to be a great coach—I felt on my own. And my self-doubt started harassing me again.

Eighty-five miles an hour. That's it? Nobody makes the Major Leagues with that kind of speed. My grandma could hit off that.

I knew the scouts looked for ninety plus, because fastballs in the eighties are actually hit-able. It's nothing special. But ninety and above with a good breaking pitch—and I had a really good curveball—*that's* what they were looking for. When I threw, I gave 100 percent effort. I mean, I gave it everything I had. If I'm a 100 percent effort guy and I'm only throwing eighty-six, I saw it clearly—*It's not going to happen.*

Worse was that the media had noticed too. Some reporters were showing up now during our practices—something they had never done before. Then they'd grab a coach, the other players, or me and ask about the upcoming record, my surgery, or how I felt pitching. They continually mentioned that my pitching had changed, slowed. They believed I'd come back, they wrote, because they saw how hard I had been working. But in my mind, the fears pressed in on me—*I'm not ever going to get back up to what I was.* Even so, I still held out hope that my dream wasn't over. Maybe not the major leagues, but the minor leagues? I did not care, as long as I got to continue playing baseball.

Then my elbow started getting sore.

The last thing on my mind was now the national record—I wondered if I could win even one game! But I was determined to do everything I could to make it happen.

Our first game finally arrived. We played Class 5A Alief Hastings Bears at Fireman's Park in Brenham. Alief is a suburb of Houston. If we won this game, it would be my twenty-ninth consecutive win. My shoulder and elbow felt okay. I did extra warm ups, I remembered to do my exercises and stretches. Now it was time to see what I really had in me.

I stood on the mound, wound up, and threw the ball. Strike! Inwardly, I was jumping and shouting for joy. I still had my mojo!

Batter after batter came and went. Strikes all.

By the fifth inning, though, my arm started to lose its pinpoint accuracy. Coach Hathaway called the pitches and the catcher relayed them to me. But Coach changed up what I was used to. I shrugged, but decided to follow his lead. The batter eyed me nervously and swung at the ball with all his might. *Crack!* He connected with it. And boy was I mad! Then I struggled even more with placing the ball and ended up walking two more batters. What could have been—what *should* have been—a shutout ended up giving the opposing team three runs.

We still won 13-3, with the game ending after six innings because of the ten-run rule (if your team has a ten-run advantage, you end the game early).

"Sorry about that, Jon," Coach Hathaway told me after the game. "I didn't set up the changeup very well and it messed you up. I take the blame for that."

I was pretty annoyed about it, but I tried to focus on the fact that at least we won—and my arm didn't give out on me.

The next game? My arm was a little tender, but again, we won. And again and again. Our winning streak continued. Even though my pitching speed wasn't at the top, it still seemed to be fast and strong enough to do what I set out to do. That realization increased my hope that perhaps I could still make it to the majors.

With each win came the influx of requests for interviews. Reporters were coming out of the woodwork, it seemed! Everywhere I was, there they were too, determined to cover the story in detail. It reminded me of a group of buzzards flying over their prey. Regardless of my many attempts to sneak away, they found me. After all, there weren't too many places to hide in a small town of only about eleven thousand people. It did not take long before I gave in and learned to go with the flow.

Within the community, it was more of the same. As I went out to do what high school kids do—date, hang out with friends— eyes stared at me and conversations turned to a whispering hum. From near and far, people intently watched my every move. If my eyes met theirs, they glanced away quickly as if they were looking somewhere else. I did not feel in sync with people, and the longer the awkwardness continued, the more my shoulders were weighted down. The hopes of the entire community felt like a ton of bricks. I did not want to disappoint them—not as I had done with the Junior Olympics.

At home I'm sure my parents worried over the constant media attention or the comments about their son. Although we did not talk much about the winning streak or the fast approaching national tie-breaking record, I knew they were excited for me.

It's possible they thought they would jinx me by talking about the record—baseball is a very superstitious sport—or perhaps they just did not know what to say. Maybe they knew my patience was wearing thin from all the attention and they did not want to be the target of my temperamental outbursts, which I still struggled over. I guess we were all trying to find our way through something none of us had experienced before.

By win number thirty-three and the record tied, the community began to prepare for what was to be the biggest sporting event in town history. Would I beat Mike Pill's record from 1975-1977 in West Covina, California? There was no social media in the late 1980s. Radio, television, and print media was all we had. And now I had gotten the national media's attention.

I tried to act cool about it, but it began to consume my every thought. Of course I still had to win the game and break the record. Everything was contingent on that.

The night before the game I was feeling edgy, so I called my buddy Jeff. The one person, besides Jill, who grounded me and who I could really talk about this stuff with was Jeff. Only, Jeff's leukemia had flared up again and he was in Houston at Texas Children's Hospital. So every night either he would call me or I'd call him. This night I called him.

"Hey, what's going on in Brenham?" he said, as soon as he heard my voice. "Place all crazy for tomorrow's game? ESPN going to be there?" His voice sounded upbeat but weak.

That was Jeff. He was always upbeat. He didn't want to focus on the disease. He wanted to *live* and experience life through his friends.

"Aw, Jeff, I ain't worried about ESPN. I want to hear about you."

"No, I want to know what's going on."

So we talked a little about what happened at school and how the teachers were and how much homework they piled on.

"Jon, you're going to do it tomorrow. You're going to beat that record."

"Well, I don't care—"

"You're *going* to beat it," he said, cutting me off. "I wish I could be there to see it for myself. Tell me all about it, okay?"

I promised I would. I got off the phone feeling as if life were unfair. Jeff should have been healthy. He should be playing right next to me, instead of stuck in a hospital bed and getting second-hand news.

I crawled into bed and willed myself to sleep. Even though I was excited about the next day and what it held, I knew I needed to get rest. I rubbed my elbow. "Don't fail me tomorrow," I told it.

Early the next morning I pulled into my school's parking lot and parked my car. As soon as I got out, I spotted Jill running toward me.

"Hey, babe!" she said as she ran up to me and kissed me.

Every game day, Jill and I had a ritual. When we first started dating, she gave me a gold necklace with a "21" pendant on it—since 21 was my baseball number. So every morning of a game, she and I would meet in the parking lot before school and I'd give her that necklace to wear.

"You're going to be great," she told me and kissed me again.

I looked at her and smiled. Her blonde hair was curled and she'd placed ribbons in her hair, something she always wore. She was wearing our school colors—green and white—to show her school spirit. And around her neck hung that necklace—to show the world she belonged to number 21. I loved her.

We walked hand in hand into the school building before our first class started, then we parted ways. But that game day ritual got me through the day. I knew somebody cared about me for me, not just because I could play baseball.

This day, though, even Jill's support was not enough to calm my nerves. I walked through the school halls trying *not* to think about this potentially being the biggest day of my life. Amid the excitement, those pesky self-doubts returned. *What if this is the one game I fail on? What will the media write about me—that I did so well all the way until the game that counted, and then I blew it? What will everybody think and say about me? What if my shoulder gives out, just as it did at the Junior Olympics?*

The day was the longest, slowest day of my life. When the final bell rang, signaling the end of classes, I rushed out of my seat. I had important rituals to handle before the game!

The players had to be at the field at 5 o'clock, so I had just less than two hours to get ready. First I drove to McDonald's and got a Big Mac. Then I went to Jill's house, which was in town and closer to the field. Even though she was still back at school and I was alone at her house (her parents liked and trusted me), I ate there, hung out and relaxed until I needed to get dressed. I'd put on my uniform there, and then head over to the field for warmups.

Fireman's Park was the community's park and ball field where the high school played all its games. It was always crowded on game days, but as I pulled up to park, I blinked hard and looked again. The field and the surrounding areas were covered with cars and people. Reporters were often there, but this time reporters were joined by giant cameras, all pointing toward the mound in the middle of the baseball diamond.

Don't think about that, just focus, I told myself as I grabbed my gear and headed toward the field where some of the other players were already hanging out.

"Look at it all!" a player said, laughing and in awe. "This is crazy!"

"I know," I said and laughed too. And it was. This was all for some *high school* kid!

"Okay, guys, let's huddle around," Coach Hathaway said once all our team was present. "Obviously this is a big game." He glanced at me and nodded. "But I don't want you to pay attention to the cameras and all the hoopla going on out there. You stay focused on the game. Give it everything you've got. If you play like you've been playing—and like I know you can—then we'll win this one too. Now take a lap!"

We all ran around the whole field and then headed over to the left field area where we stretched. Most of my teammates seemed to enjoy the attention.

"I heard *Sports Illustrated* is coming. Do you think that's true?"

"I think ESPN is here. Is that them?"

"Look at all those reporters!"

I tried to act the part too, but it made me uncomfortable. I just wanted to play the game and not have to worry about that side of it.

With our stretches and throwing warmups complete, we headed back in for batting practice.

People kept pouring into the stands and the noise level rose. Cheers and chants and yells—all for the Brenham High School Cubs.

"Let's go Cubbies!"

"We gotta win this one!"

"Let's do this, boys!"

"Make us proud!"

We were playing the Oak Ridge War Eagles from Conroe, just north of Houston, about seventy miles east of Brenham.

As they warmed up, I realized what a terrible position they were in. Basically everybody—the whole media included—were rooting for them to lose. And so was I. The butterflies had reappeared in my stomach and I felt nauseated by the whole thing, but I knew once the game started, once I was on the mound with the clay dirt beneath my feet, once I held the pearl and gripped it tightly in my hands, everything would be okay. This was my turf. My people. My home. This was my time.

My arm was feeling good. It loosened up just as I needed it to. And I knew we were going to win. I was going to dominate. With each throw, the ball still went exactly where I wanted it to go.

At the top of the first inning, the top of the game, I stepped onto the mound and breathed in deeply. In the background I could hear the crowd yelling in excitement and anticipation, but I blocked them out. I kicked at the dirt on the mound and played with it a bit, smoothing it out. Then I stood straight and faced my catcher. It was go time. With another deep breath, I stared intently at the first batter up. Poor guy. I was going to crush him. I almost felt sorry for him. Almost.

I wound up, feeling my arm come alive. It felt fresh and strong. The release came fast and hard. *Strike!*

The crowd went crazy.

Strike!

Strike—out!

The batters came up and went down.

Yeah, I still got it, I thought, feeling cocky now that my nerves were under control.

The game flew by, and my arm kept feeling stronger and stronger. I couldn't lose. And everybody knew it.

The game ended with a winning 5-0 score. I struck out the first thirteen of fifteen batters and gave up only one hit that came in the top of the seventh inning with one out. I was the new national record holder for most consecutive wins by a high school pitcher—thirty-four. Now our team and community could focus on what we had really set our sights on at the beginning of the season: taking our third consecutive state championship!

This night, this game, however, was still something to celebrate. And celebrate we did. The players and coaches huddled around the mound giving one another bone-crushing bear hugs, high-fives, and vice-grip handshakes. The horde of photographers had rushed the field and was snapping photos at lightning speed, while the crowd roared with chants and yells reaching dangerous decibel levels. The media sprinted onto the field as well to ask questions and capture the reactions of the players and coaches. The record books had just been rewritten. History was no longer in the making; it had been made.

I felt pulled and pushed from every direction as people grabbed at me to offer hugs and congratulations. In the midst of the throng, Coach Hathaway reached over and took my arm to lead me through the crowd. Our hometown radio station, KWHI, had been so good to us through all the seasons, we wanted to give back and offer them an interview. So Coach and I headed up to the booth at the top of the stands. As I looked down on the field, I was amazed by all the celebrating taking place. And as the radio announcer chatted with me about the record, I tried to sound as mature and upbeat as possible. I thanked them for their constant support. I praised our coaches and my teammates, insisting that it wasn't me alone who won that game. Everyone played an important role. Each question brought a positive and upbeat answer. But each question kept me from what I really wanted to be doing.

As soon as the interview was over, I snuck down the bleacher steps and into the dugout, where I reached into my bag and grabbed a phone calling card. Then I headed to the right field area, where just beyond the stadium stood a pay-phone. Using the card for payment, I called Texas Children's Hospital.

The battle we had fought on the field was nothing compared to the battle my friend Jeff was fighting at the hospital. The opponent he was competing against was more powerful and relentless, persistently coming back for more. It was not quitting, and regardless of what the doctors threw at it, it was not going away.

I couldn't beat his opponent as I had beaten mine, but I could share the celebration with him.

The phone rang and soon I heard, "Hello?"

"Jeff, we won!"

"Man, I knew it. I knew it! Tell me all about it! Don't leave out anything."

We talked about the game—the thousands of people in attendance; the news reporters, the writers and cameramen from ESPN, *Sports Illustrated,* and other affiliates; the pregame festivities; the first pitch; the first run; the amount of food and drink the concession prepared; and the postgame celebration. I shared about it all, and he listened and asked questions. We laughed about how crazy and different life had become and how we were looking forward to some sense of normalcy in the days ahead. It was like he was there at the park with me and he had experienced it all.

"Enough about the game," I finally said. "How are you doing?" I just wanted to hear about him and what was going on in his world. Even during this most exciting time, I wanted to feel some normalcy. The attention had been on me for so long that I was beginning to play into it, and that was never a good thing. Thinking about myself all day was making me miserable. Jeff was good at pulling me out of that mess. He had a way of putting life into perspective. And that was something I needed.

He shared with me about his day, the prognosis the doctors had given him and the treatment planned. It did not sound good. How he kept fighting continued to be a mystery to me. It seemed like the longer and harder the fight grew, the more determined Jeff became in eliminating the disease.

Things were starting to quiet down on the field as people took their celebrating back to town or to their homes. I was going to hook up with Jill and catch a bite to eat with her, so we wound down our conversation.

"Hey, Jon," Jeff said, before we offered our good-byes. "I'm proud of you."

A lump swelled in my throat. This kid who was going through hell was so selfless. I did not deserve his friendship. This conversation right there, right then, was the best thing about this whole day.

"I love you, man," I choked out.

At that moment, the whirl of life stopped. Jeff didn't have leukemia. I was not the national record holder. We were just two friends who deeply mattered to each other. That was better than all the records and fame and media attention.

CHAPTER 10

NOT QUITE THE NATIONAL RECORD

Just a little more and it will be over, I kept telling myself on Saturday morning. Less than twelve hours after breaking the record, I was back in my green Cubs uniform and on the pitcher's mound at Fireman's Park. Over and over I pretended to throw the ball so the photographer could get just the right angle and expression. My arm was hurting and I was getting frustrated. *How many photos does this guy need to take?*

As if reading my mind, he said, "I know this seems like a lot, but we want to make sure we get just the right one in the event you make the cover."

Wait. What? Sports Illustrated *may feature me on the cover?* I was stunned. When their writer interviewed me earlier in the week and then again right after the game, he never mentioned anything about a cover story. I just figured it would be a blip in the back of the magazine somewhere. I knew the record was a big deal, but I did not think it might be such a big deal to be on the *cover* of *Sports Illustrated.* My jaw dropped. *Really? Why me? I'm just a junior in high school.*

I pushed thoughts of my aching arm to the back of my mind and nodded to him as if his announcement were no big deal.

"I think we have a good shot at it," he said.

I nodded again. "That would be such an honor," I told him, meaning it, but still astonished that a high schooler—me—would even be *considered* for the cover of one of my favorite magazines.

A few days later, as I walked into the stadium for our daily practice, Coach Hathaway said, "Hey, Jon, come over here for a minute. I want to talk with you about something."

What's up this time? I wondered. I knew it wasn't news about a national record, since I'd already won that! What else could it be?

He nodded and waved me over.

"I heard from a reporter today—"

Here we go again, I thought, feeling my blood pressure rise. I was tired of reporters. I figured once I had beaten the national record, I would be in the limelight for a little while and then life would move on and the reporters would lose interest. But that did not happen. Their interest in me seemed endless. And I was growing weary of the constant requests for interviews. I just wanted to be a normal teenager. I was exhausted from pretending to be someone I really wasn't. With all the attention on me, I had to diligently monitor how I acted most of the time so my good ol' boy, all-American reputation was not tarnished.

My angry outbursts were still a problem for me, but I had learned how to keep them from public view. But even that was difficult when a reporter would harass me for information and all I really wanted to tell them was to get lost—but in more colorful language. Now Coach was telling me about some *other* reporter.

"*Sports Illustrated* called today," Coach continued. "The story they are doing is going to make the cover."

My breath caught in my throat. The cover was really happening!

"They plan to call you sometime this week with the details. I just wanted to give you the heads up and congratulate you. That's a big deal, Jon."

Yeah, he didn't have to tell me that. I *knew* it was a big deal. *Sports Illustrated* covered all my baseball heroes—the big guys. But *me*? *And* for the cover? I would be the first high school baseball player to make the front of the magazine. I tried to act cool, but inside, I was doing flips!

Sure enough, a few days later, the phone rang.

"Jon!" my mom's voice rang out from the kitchen. "Phone."

As I raced to get it, she whispered, "*Sports Illustrated.*" My heart skipped a beat.

The reporter congratulated me again on the record. "It's confirmed. We're going to put you on the cover."

"Thank you, sir, that is an honor," I said, then added, "and just being in the magazine is honor enough too."

That week I was all the buzz. Everyone in town knew about *Sports Illustrated*'s visit and it seemed that was all anybody cared to discuss. Amid the congratulations, though, I had a few folks remind me of the jinx connected with being on the cover.

"Oh, Jon, you know bad luck follows athletes who show up on the cover," some would say and shake their heads.

"Yeah, I know," I'd reply and try to smile it off.

The jinx was that an athlete was on the cover one day, and the next, his playing days were over. Enough athletes had experienced it that people began to connect the two and called it a jinx. I did not really believe it though.

Even though I knew it was an honor and I kept pinching myself to make sure this was all not a dream, a small part of me still cringed at what I was sure it would bring with it—more publicity, more of me not being just a normal kid, playing a game I loved.

Will they ever leave me alone? I am so tired of everyone watching me. Those thoughts mingled with the darker thoughts that were my constant companion. *I am not as good as they think I am.* My doubts of self-worth, lack of confidence, and fear of failure were at an all-time high. It didn't matter that it didn't make sense; I had broken a record. I was a good player. Still, the thoughts plagued me—and I believed them.

Several days later, a large envelope arrived in the mail addressed to me. The return address blazed *Sports Illustrated*. This was it! I ripped open the top of the package and pulled out a one-page flyer of how the cover would look. It was dated May 9, 1988, and was attached to the current weekly edition of the magazine that was in circulation at the local newsstands. The title was "Kid K"—"K" standing for "strike out. The subtitle announced, "Texas High School Pitching Phenom Jon Peters." And the photo showed me on the mound, leaning forward, having just thrown a ball.

The advertising promotion kick-started the fanfare in the community as people eagerly awaited the release. Although I had many doubts, I was looking forward to it as well. It was going to be a great ending to a great story.

Several days later, while sitting in English class, a knock came and the door slowly opened. Mr. McCarson, our principal, was peeking in.

"Can I speak with Jon for a moment?"

Mr. McCarson never asked to see anybody unless something serious or bad had happened. Thirty sets of eyes turned in my direction as I tried to maneuver out of my desk and walk toward him. I swallowed hard. I hadn't acted up in a long time. Everything had been peaceful, quiet. Why did he want to see me?

Maybe it isn't bad, I told myself. Maybe a television station like ESPN wanted to interview me. Yes, I was sure that was it.

He motioned quietly for me to follow him. Without a word between us, we walked down the long hall, past classroom after classroom. He seemed awkward, reserved, and I got the funny feeling this wasn't about a television interview.

My stomach started to feel queasy as we approached his office. Then I became confused when he walked right by it. "Am I in trouble?" I finally asked.

He smiled tightly and put his hand on my shoulder. With a firm squeeze, he said, "You did not do anything wrong. I want to talk with you about this baseball record."

I nodded but was still confused. *The record is done and over with. And the magazine will soon be coming out. What else can we discuss?*

Onward we went, through the outside doors until we reached the steps in front of the school where he indicated we should sit.

"Jon, you've done an amazing job this year," he said. "You had that injury and you worked hard and came back strong. And I'm so proud of you with the way you handled breaking the record with gratitude and humility. I'm most proud that regardless of how good a pitcher you are, you are an even better young man, and that says a lot about your character."

I nodded, knowing that the character stuff was not nearly as solid as he thought it was. But it meant a lot hearing him say it.

Then he shared with me about some of the behind-the-scenes activities I was not aware of. For instance, he told me about the time a reporter was adamant about talking with me during school hours and he slammed the door in his face and threatened to call the police. We talked as if we had all day with nothing better to do. But the longer he talked, the more uncomfortable I started to feel and I realized he was not just chatting to chat, he had something serious to tell me and he didn't know how to do it.

His demeanor became gentle, like a father delivering disappointing news to his son. He nervously stuttered, "There appears to have been a mistake made. Someone at the National Federation of High School Sports discovered that a pitcher from South Carolina won fifty straight games in the early '80s. For some reason, it had never been reported." He paused and inhaled deeply. "So . . . the record of thirty-four is not a record. It's actually fifty."

I hadn't broken the record.

As I listened to his words and gazed into his eyes trying to comprehend what I had just heard, flashbacks of the past few months began to flood my mind. It started with a calm, peaceful stream and quickly moved to a raging, out-of-control tsunami. All the hoopla and celebrations and interviews—all of it was for nothing. All the great experiences I had shared with some of my best friends and my greatest fans. The opportunities of a lifetime I had, believing them to be great memories for the future. Instead I had played just another game.

Now I wanted to be left alone.

"You'll be able to try again next year," Mr. McCarson said in an encouraging tone.

I nodded blankly and tried to look unaffected. But I couldn't believe it. *How was a mistake like this made? How did someone not catch this sooner? Everybody drove me crazy for the past few months for* this*? Everybody in the country was reporting the record and they just happened to find out about it* now*? Are you kidding me? This is ridiculous! What a nightmare!*

We stared at each other silently. Finally, I spoke, followed by a sarcastic laugh. "That's, like, sixteen more wins. There's no way. That's not going to happen. I guess it was fun while it lasted."

We continued talking about the days leading up to the record. But inside I felt chaotic. I was ready to go. I had heard enough. We slowly rose and started back toward the building.

"Jon, there is one more thing," he said.

"Yes sir, what's that?"

"You may know that Pete Rose got into an argument and bumped an umpire the other day."

I nodded. I had heard about Cincinnati Reds' Pete Rose's altercation that led to a thirty-day suspension.

"*Sports Illustrated* has decided to put him on the cover," Mr. McCarson said. "But they're still going to run your story in the magazine."

I opened the door, and without a word, I walked down the hallway back to my classroom.

I had not broken the national record *and* I was getting pulled from the *Sports Illustrated* cover. All in one day.

For all my acting like those things were not a big deal, losing them broke my heart.

CHAPTER 11
DEVASTATING NEWS

"Gee, Jon, sorry about not making the cover of *Sports Illustrated*."

"Oh, Jon, that's too bad about not breaking the record. Maybe next year."

Over and over I heard people's comments, and the more I heard them—even well meaning—the angrier I grew. I didn't want their pity. I didn't want the attention. I just wanted to be left alone.

It didn't seem to matter to people that we won our third consecutive state baseball championship, or that my record at the end of my junior year stood at forty-two consecutive wins. Sure, they celebrated with us, but always with a side comment about perhaps breaking the record next season or showing *Sports Illustrated* how wrong they were. In other words, nobody seemed content to let my failings die, they had to continually bring them up and remind me.

That added to the pressure I was feeling moving into my senior year. Possibly breaking the record for real and carrying all the expectations that came with that. Going for a fourth consecutive state championship, and carrying all the expectations that came with *that*. And looking at colleges with an eye to playing baseball, and carrying all the expectations that came with that too.

So whenever someone said something that I felt slighted me or set me on edge, I was cocked and ready to go. Cursing them out in my head, I would smile tightly at them and shrug it off, but I could not let the comment go. And I didn't know how to handle it properly, so I took it out on those closest to me. I would snap over the smallest, most insignificant things. My parents took the brunt of it. So did Jill.

I loved Jill, as much as any teenager can love another person. But I could never get over the idea that she might love me in return. She was the most beautiful girl in school. Jill was tall, tan, and had beautiful blonde hair. She was athletic and ranked number one on the girls' high school tennis team. She was outgoing with the sweetest, most bubbly personality. And whenever I was with her, she doted on me. I felt lucky to be with her.

So why could I never quite believe she really cared for me? I was certain I was never good enough for her. In my mind, I still saw myself as the fat, awkward kid—and I knew at some point, she was going to find out the truth. So I would pick fights with her to prove I was right—that she was faking her love.

From the outside, all our friends thought Jill and I were the perfect couple, that things were good between us. And they were, as long as I didn't sabotage our relationship with my insecurities. I was so afraid of getting hurt, of being vulnerable, or her rejecting me, that I treated her with disrespect. I knew it was stupid when I did those things! But I just couldn't stop myself.

And she never knew when I would blow up. Like the time she came with me and my family to Houston when my cousin got married. We had a great time. At the end of the evening, as we were leaving the reception, Jill slapped me on my backside, sort of a playful, *Come on, big boy. Let's go.*

Immediately I turned on her. "What are you hitting me for?"

She stood, stunned and speechless at how quickly I had turned angry and ugly toward her.

"Y'all go on by yourself," I told my family.

"But how are you going to get back home?" Jill asked.

"Don't worry about it. I'll find a way." I walked away, not sure where I was or where I was going, but I was so furious that she had done that to me that I didn't care. I knew my family would look for me, but I called a friend, who picked me up and drove me home. I did not care that I had just ruined a great evening.

Later that year on Thanksgiving during my senior year, I was at Jill's house watching football. It was the big showdown game between The University of Texas and Texas A&M. While everybody was rooting for the Aggies (Texas A&M), I was the sole hold-out for the Longhorns (UT). I loved that school and planned to attend there the following year to play baseball for them.

The University of Texas wasn't doing so well during the game and everybody started teasing me. It was all in good fun.

"Uh oh, Jon, your precious UT is going down!"

"Oops, another interception. Poor baby, Jon."

Everyone was laughing and I was okay being the butt of their jokes—for a while. But then I started to get annoyed, forgetting that it was teasing. I felt they were being serious. I could take it from others, but Jill was joining in.

Finally, I'd had enough.

"Stop picking on me!" I yelled. "What is wrong with you people?" I grabbed my letterman jacket and flung it as hard as I could across the room. The sleeve smacked into her mother's cuckoo clock and broke it. I felt bad, but I was so steamed by this point that I wouldn't apologize. I gave Jill a dirty look, as if she were at fault, and then I stormed out of her house.

"Jon, wait!" Jill yelled, running after me.

I turned fast to face her. "You're supposed to be on my side. You are supposed to support me, not make a fool out of me with everybody else in there. Just stay away from me." I turned on my heel, away from her, and left.

Things stayed tense for a while, but eventually everything calmed down. And I never apologized for the clock incident. *They made me do it* was my rationale.

But the next time I saw Jill's mom, she refused to let my behavior go. "Jon, you need to go get some help."

"What do you mean?"

"Something is not firing right in your brain," she told me. "You just snap and that's not normal."

Nobody had ever confronted me like that before. My parents hadn't. I knew she was right, but I didn't know how to stop it. To my way of thinking, I just needed to not consider it and move on as though nothing had happened. But deep down, when they were teasing about the college's poor performance on the football field, I took it that they were commenting on me personally. And that fed into my already fragile ego—not that I could articulate that!

I listened respectfully to Jill's mom, I agreed internally, but nothing changed. I continued to allow my temper to rule me. Then not long after, my dad and I were sitting together in our kitchen and Jill came up in our conversation. My dad casually said, "There are plenty of fish in the sea. If it's meant to be, it will be."

I didn't know what that meant. Was he suggesting that someone my age was supposed to date multiple girls at the same time? That sounded wrong, and surely someone's feelings were to get hurt. Did it mean to keep my options open? If so, how was I supposed to give 100 percent of myself in this relationship with Jill? As with baseball, I was either all in or all out; that was my personality.

I was not about to ask questions because that would reveal my ignorance of dating, plus I did not want to appear to question Dad's knowledge and advice, so I stayed silent.

My dad had never led me astray before, and surely this was not to be the first time. He was my biggest fan and supporter. But something about what he said stuck with me, and eventually, I realized what I needed to do.

Sitting at the kitchen table at Jill's house, my heart was breaking and my eyes were filling with tears. I did not want to say what I had rehearsed so many times in my mind. I tried to convince myself it was going to turn out fine, but my heart knew better.

"I think we should break up," I told her, watching her face drain of its color and her eyes grow big and watery. "We should see other people. You know, to make sure we're a good fit." I could not look at her face, knowing how much I was hurting her, hurting me. "We can get back together down the road if that is where it leads us. But for right now, I think it's better for us to date others."

It took all I had to stutter those words. I did not want that, but I was unable to remove the "voice of reason" from my head, the protective covering I had placed over me. As the tears flowed down her beautiful face, the emotional scars of shame and guilt began to fill my soul. I had just deeply wounded the heart of an amazing girl I loved. I had created this all. It was 100 percent me.

I left her house and refused to look back. *It's better this way*, I said to console myself.

Only, it was not better. I was more miserable than I had ever been in my life. And in some warped way, I was relieved to know Jill was just as miserable.

A few days later, Jill and I were talking again, and shortly after, we were back together. I felt as though my heart was full again and she seemed the same way. She was so good at forgiving me. I wished I were as good at forgiving myself.

Instead of being content and grateful with the "now," I kept holding on to regrets from the past while constantly worrying about the future. *I'm not good enough. I don't fit in. Jill doesn't really like me. She's just being nice.*

Soon I was back to my old ways. I had become the "master of sabotage" by routinely and unexpectedly altering my behavior for no apparent reason. It did not matter if things were going well. Others would have to walk on eggshells because they never knew what I was capable of. One minute things would be great, with smiles and laughter, and the next would be filled with rage and anger. I didn't know why, nor did I like it. In one breath I was calm, peaceful, and fun to be around. With the next breath I was irritated and discontent. The people who knew me shrugged it off and blamed it on my lack of maturity, but I knew it was more than that.

Though we never dated anyone else, I had created a pattern of distrust and a lack of loyalty. The problem was *me*—pride and fear stood in the way and it would take a miracle to minimize that giant, much less remove it.

So once again, I would approach Jill and tell her we needed our space. I would give the usual "so we can date other people" along with new rationales—"I have colleges to consider and the season is gearing up to start. I have a lot of pressure on me."

She would cry and beg me not to do it, but some stupid sense of power came over me. I hated hurting her, but I could not explain why I was doing it—when we both knew we didn't want to break up.

And as the cycle continued, within a few days, we would once again be back together.

I was glad we were together when the baseball season started—especially since we had our rituals, which by now had become superstitions to me. Each morning of a game, she met me in the school parking lot and I gave her my "21" necklace to wear for good luck. It had never failed me, and I definitely needed it this season.

The big question around town and the state was, "Can Brenham repeat as state champions for the fourth year in a row?" We were returning quite a few players from the previous year and if everything went according to plan, the answer to that question would be a resounding yes.

The chitter-chatter of the national record was also slowly creeping back, although the media had backed off somewhat. If I was able to win a few more games, I had a realistic chance of breaking the record.

The season started just like the previous years. We racked up win after win, dominating many of our opponents. The excitement was growing even greater than before.

Win number forty-seven. Win number forty-eight. Win number forty-nine. Win number fifty. This was it. One more win.

It was all coming down to one spring night in April 1989. The script had been written and the show had been rehearsed once before, almost exactly one year to the date. It had gone off without many hitches, but this time the show was real. The current record holder, Timmy Moore, from South Carolina, was even scheduled to make an appearance. This was the real deal.

Thursday, the day before the game, I got ready to head to practice and thought about how different this record was compared to the previous one. If I broke it, everybody would be excited, the media would go crazy, the town would rejoice, but one important person would be missing from the festivities. Just a short year prior, my friend, Jeff, had fought leukemia so hard and had celebrated with me when I'd "broken" the record the first time. Now his fight was over. He died on January 18, 1989, just a few months past, and I still felt the void of his friendship. Even if I broke the record, the celebration wouldn't be the same.

"Jeff, buddy, I wish you were here to see this." I sighed. I couldn't think about that loss now. I needed to focus on the task ahead. I knew, though, that if he were alive, he would be rooting for me, supporting me. I missed him.

I tried to put it out of my mind as I headed to baseball practice. When I arrived at the field, the media were already there, setting up, trying to get interviews and day-before shots. I wasn't sure what exactly they thought they'd get that would be so amazing. It was just a typical practice, just shorter. Compared to every other practice, our day-before-game practices were relaxed and loose for both the coaches and the players. They included a pregame infield and outfield—in which each player assumes his position and the coach hits groundballs and flyballs to the players, which they catch and then throw to other players to replicate specific game plays, such as a double play or a pop-up. We followed that up with a normal round of batting practice.

As we were practicing this day, I started to sense a weird vibe from some of the players. They were talking quietly and every once in a while, I would catch my name. As practice was nearing an end, my curiosity got the best of me.

"What's up?" I asked one of my teammates.

He squirmed a little but then admitted what the guys had been discussing. "Jill was with another guy."

"What? When? *Now?*" I felt panicked, but tried to keep calm.

"No, a couple months ago." He and some of the other guys started to tell me the gossip. It wasn't just that she had gone on a date with "some" guy; he was a good friend of mine. The news was ugly and hurtful. The things I overheard were alarming and enough to make my temperature boil, and I knew I had to get away before my temper emerged. It did not matter that she had dated someone else while we were on a break—something *I* had insisted on. It did not matter that *I* had cheated on her the previous year. I never imagined she would actually accept my proposal for her to date other people! My mind went into overdrive after hearing the story, concocting and projecting every possibility.

I had to get out of there before I exploded. I forced myself to calm down and managed to act cool for the brief remainder of the practice. But as soon as practice was over, I rushed to my car and headed home.

No, I told myself. *It can't be true. They're just making stuff up. The rumors are just to get me agitated before tomorrow's game, that's all.*

By the time I arrived home, I had talked myself into believing that the guys were wrong. I took a quick shower and then headed over to my friend Kevin Picone's house for pizza and a few games of eight-ball pool with him and another friend, Steven Gurka. This was another of my superstitions—ball players are some of the most superstitious people around—and since it was working, I figured there was no reason to change it. Before every game I pitched, my friends and I would gather at Kevin's house, which also happened to belong to my math teacher and her husband. They were my "parental cheerleaders" and they supported and encouraged me, not only in baseball but in anything I participated in. If I needed a boost of energy or just a pat on the back, they always provided that.

I was not very good at pool as I lacked the finesse and delicate touch to roll each ball into the pockets. I was like that with a lot of things—similar to a bull in a china closet in that I wanted to power-drive the balls into each hole, hitting them as hard as possible. But every now and then I got on a roll making several good shots, although I seldom won many games. That was okay with me because it was more of a night to have fun and relax. It turned my mind off the thoughts of the upcoming game—and of the news I had just heard. Something I desperately needed.

Kevin's house and our pool and pizza ritual had become a haven for me, a safe place. This night, however, the haven was to be split wide open since the writer for *Sports Illustrated* and his camera crew would be joining us. Once again, I was going to have to put on my game face and pretend everything was fine, even though I felt as though I was in the middle of dying a slow and painful death.

"Jon!" Mr. and Mrs. Picone greeted me at the door and gave me a hug. "Come in, come in. The *Sports Illustrated* people are already here and setting up. Pizza is on its way."

"Great," I muttered and tried to pass it off with a smile.

As we ate pizza and played numerous games of eight-ball, the writer asked all of us questions and his crew took photos to capture the evening. The questions were not all about baseball and the record. Many were about the community, friends, family, and everyday type of stuff. He was just "one of the guys" and soon I began to let down my guard. There were even times when we laughed and all agreed, "It's probably best to keep that out of the article." But still lurking in the back of my mind was the gossip I had heard earlier in the day.

Was it true? What really happened? Had I lost the love of my life?

As the gathering was ending and we prepared to call it a night, the writer talked about his earlier conversations during the day with people in the community, our families and friends, our coaches and teammates—and Jill. He looked at me as if waiting to see how I would respond. I refused to give him the satisfaction and acted like I hadn't heard anything.

Everybody knew, except me. What a fool I had been.

As soon as the party was over, I headed to Jill's house for a showdown. I had to hear it directly from her.

Jill's mother greeted me at the back door with a smile, but after seeing the look on my face, her smile quickly faded. "Jill's in her room," she said, now looking surprised and concerned. "You can go on back."

I was so upset, I didn't even thank her. I just nodded and headed through the kitchen and down the hallway to Jill's bedroom.

"Is it true what I hear about you and my friend?" I said as soon as I entered her room.

She was sitting on her bed, reading. Her face went pale, and I knew then that it was. But still, I wanted to hear her admit it. Admit that she had gone out with my good friend.

She put down her book. "What did you hear?"

"Look, I know what happened. If you tell me the truth, we'll stay together. But if you lie to me, it's over."

Slowly she inhaled. "What you heard is true."

I felt furious. *Really? I can't believe you did this to me,* I thought. I wanted to destroy everything in her house!

"We're done." Before she could react, I turned and walked out of her room and straight out of her house. I got into my car and let the tears flow down my cheeks.

That was my MO. Instead of facing things and working through them, when things got too difficult, I wanted to quit. When my Little League team wasn't winning, when the Junior Olympic try-outs were too intimidating, when my relationships became messy, I ran away from everything. Now I was going to run away for the last time.

I reached up to my neck and felt the gold chain with the "21" pendant hanging there. It felt like an anchor. Jill had given me that necklace and our tradition had been for me to place it on her every game day morning as a good luck charm. It didn't feel so lucky at this moment.

As I allowed the tears to flow, between forceful gasps of air, I sincerely prayed for the first time in my life.

"God, I'm done," I said out loud. "I'm tired of all this. Just take me. Just let me die. I am so tired of trying to be somebody for everyone. I do *not* want this. I do *not* deserve this. I do *not* want all this attention. I am really *not* that good. I couldn't care less about this record. I just want to be normal. All I want to do is be happy, to be a normal kid who gets to act like a kid. Everyone is so wrapped up in this media stuff. I have been crying out for help for so long. No one is listening. I cannot handle this. I am in so much pain and I hurt so freaking bad. Please. Please make it go away. I am so done. I'm done with baseball, done with relationships. And I am done with life. Done."

Through the sobs I tried to think about ways I could end it. End the pain, end the expectations on me, end the burden of being someone I wasn't, end the insecurity, end it all. I just wanted it all to be over.

I thought about swerving the car off the road and hitting a tree, but I was too chicken. My dad had a shotgun for hunting, so I thought that might work, but then I talked myself out of that option. *What if I don't die? I'd be in even worse shape.* I considered slitting my wrists, but that's too messy and painful, and I wasn't sure how to do it correctly. *Pills*, I thought. I'll take some pills and then go to sleep and never wake up. Easy.

Fifteen minutes later, at around 10:30, I parked the car and quietly entered my house, walking straight toward the kitchen cabinet where we kept the glasses. I grabbed a giant, plastic Houston Astros cup and filled it with water, grabbed the large bottle of Tylenol from another cabinet, and headed toward my bedroom.

Mom stepped out of her room to greet me. She always did that when I came home late. I tucked the Tylenol behind my back and tried to hide my face, since I knew it must be swollen from crying, but she still caught a glimpse of it. "What's wrong? What happened?"

I shrugged. "Jill and I broke up," I muttered. "I found out she went out on me with a good friend of mine." It took every ounce of determination not to break down and sob.

She grimaced. "Is she okay?"

I stopped in my tracks, stunned and hurt. *Did you really just say that? Don't you care about my pain? What are you worried about Jill for?* I wanted my mom to hold me and tell me how sorry she was, how much she wanted to take away my pain, but instead she seemed more concerned about Jill.

If I'd had even a twinge of doubt about what I was going to do, that left as soon as I heard my mom's comment. *See? She doesn't even care about me.*

Something deep inside told me that she did care, that she didn't know how to comfort me the way I needed, and that she loved me. But I didn't want to listen to that voice of reason. I just wanted to go to my room and finish what I had started.

"Well, pray to God. He will help you through this," she said. "It will be okay."

"Don't worry," I told her. "I'll be fine. Good night."

I entered my room, plopped down on the floor against the bed and looked around my room. Professional MLB pennants hung on the wall opposite me—St. Louis Cardinals, Houston Astros, Los Angeles Dodgers—along with a big poster of Nolan Ryan. *What difference did any of this make? Baseball, my dreams, Jill, my friends, God. None of it mattered. Nobody really cared.*

God. I hadn't really thought about God, even though my family and I went to church every week and even though I had not prayed to him much before that night's car ride. But even he didn't care. Where was he in all this mess? If he really loved me, as the pastor and my mother kept insisting he did, why didn't he do something to help me feel at peace and take away all this pain?

My thoughts returned to Jill. I didn't care that she had gone out with my friend while we were broken up. I didn't care that I had brought it on myself and really had no reason to be upset. How could I expect her to sit around and wait for me to make up my mind? I had taken her on an emotional rollercoaster ride of "never-know ups and never-know downs." I was lucky she still wanted to date me. But that reasoning never crossed my mind. I just hurt too much.

Did I really believe I could treat someone the way I treated her and expect no consequences? Had I really become this manipulative, controlling, and selfish monster? It sure seemed that way.

I opened the large bottle as thoughts of my whole life flashed in front of me. The teams I had been on, when I first met Jill, Coach Driggers and how he'd mentored me.

The bottle was three-quarters full. I grabbed my first pill, popped it into my mouth, and swallowed it with the water. It went down so easily.

I can't believe Jill did this to me. I popped another pill into my mouth and swallowed.

I can't believe my friend did this to me. Another pill.

What are people going to think about me when they hear about this? Another pill. I looked across the room to my desk and wondered if I should leave a note.

No, I decided. *It would serve everybody right.* Another pill.

I'm such a fake, such a loser. The pills that had started off so easy to swallow now stuck in my throat. *Great. I can't even swallow right.* I took another gulp of water and forced them down.

As I sat on the floor with my back leaning against the bed, I swallowed those pills just like I had won all of those baseball games—one after another after another until the bottle was empty. I crawled into bed. The necklace's "21" crept down the side of my neck and fell against my pillow. *Now I'll go to sleep and I won't wake up.*

I closed my eyes and waited to drift off into an eternal sleep, into final peace. I was finally done.

CHAPTER 12

SECOND CHANCES

Bong! Bong! Bong!

My head felt as if someone was repeatedly slamming it against the wall while blowing an air-horn directly into my ears. I moaned and cracked open my eyes just enough to see sunlight coming through the shutters over my bedroom windows. *Where is that noise coming from?*

I realized it was my alarm. I rolled over and smacked it to turn it off.

Great, I can't even kill myself right. I'm such a loser!

Out of habit, I must have set my alarm to wake me at 7:20—something I did every night to get me up for school. I couldn't remember setting it, though. I couldn't remember anything with the constant *eeeee* ringing in my ears. That should have stopped once I turned off the alarm, but an annoying medium-pitched ringing filled my ears and made it hard to concentrate.

So much for the newspaper headlines, I thought. When I closed my eyes the night before, I envisioned the papers announcing, "High School Pitching Phenom Dead—Suspected Overdose."

I sighed heavily. *Why does this have to happen to me? Why couldn't I just have died and be done with it all?*

I slowly forced myself out of bed, holding my ears and trying to get them to stop ringing. In the bathroom I dressed, refusing to look at myself in the mirror. I didn't want to be reminded of how much I had cried the night before.

As I walked out of the house, I noticed a few notes on the kitchen table my mom had written. She wrote me notes every morning saying things like, "Good luck! Go get 'em!" or just a simple, "I love you!" I appreciated those notes not because of what they said but because she took the time to write them. Today, though, the messages didn't mean much. Nothing mattered anymore. And I just wanted the ringing in my ears to stop!

I drove my two-door Cutlass Supreme to school and parked in the same parking spot as I always did—in front of the school, third row. I turned off the engine and sat, not wanting to face the day. Wondering if I'd see Jill. Wondering why God didn't answer my prayers. And I realized I was more of an emotional mess now than I had been the day before.

"Get it together," I told myself. "Do not cry." I bit my lip and breathed deeply, not sure how I was going to make it through the day.

As with each school day, I walked to an area at the front of the school where my friends gathered prior to the school bell ringing. My heart was so heavy. I knew at any moment I was capable of crying and falling apart. And once the tears started to flow, there was no telling when they would stop. That was the last thing I wanted to happen.

I caught sight of my friends and slowed my step. There stood Jill, looking my way. Her face betrayed a sadness and her shoulders slumped over. She looked miserable.

Hot, salty tears immediately pricked my eyes and a gasp erupted from my lips. She stood in front of me with big eyes that showed how sorry she was. I couldn't help myself; I wrapped her in my arms and cried.

Finally, I unclasped my gold necklace and held it up. She nodded, and I placed it gently around her neck. The number

"21" shone brightly against her green Cubs T-shirt. This was our tradition on game days. I didn't want to lose her. I knew how lucky I was to have her in my life—so loving, supportive, and caring—she had become my lifeline of support through thick and thin. For too long, I had taken her for granted. How could I stay angry with her?

The bell sounded for first period to begin. I wiped my eyes as we headed into the school. The hallways were filled with energy and excitement as friends yelled words of encouragement. Teachers were wearing their Cub green shirts. Posters and signs were hanging on the walls, announcing "Record breaking night" and "Come support the Cubs." Former great athletes had walked down these halls but nothing had created such a buzz as this national record. It was the biggest event that had come to town, and I was to be on center stage. If they only knew how dead inside I felt.

With each passing class period, the deep sadness grew darker. I was disgusted with the way I had acted in my relationship with Jill and I was scared of losing my first true love. Finally, just before the lunch period was to start, I excused myself from class. I was barely able to control my emotions as I raced to the rubber gym, found a quiet and private spot, and sobbed.

I don't remember how I made it through the rest of the school day. I know I didn't learn much. I know my ears kept up with that annoying *eeeee* sound. And I know I somehow smiled when people cheered me on in the hallways. I do remember what happened after school, though.

After school on game days, I would always drive to Jill's house, since it was closer to the field. I would eat my McDonald's meal there, relax for a bit, and change before heading to the game. This day, I went through the McDonald's drive-thru and ordered my usual Big Mac, French fries, and Diet Coke. This time, however, instead of driving to Jill's house, I headed to my own.

I was still bombarded with negative and accusing thoughts about how inadequate and terrible I was, I was still fighting the tears, and I just wanted to shut myself in my room and make the world go away. But I knew the world was waiting for me. They were all down at Fireman's Park, expecting me to show up and give them the excitement they'd prepared for.

I slowly put on my uniform and hat. *This is it. This is what you have worked so hard for. Jill will be there, cheering for you.* I wanted to believe that was true. I wanted to believe that I really did matter, that even if I didn't break this record, *I* would still matter.

I grabbed my keys and headed to my car. I was in no hurry to get to the ballfield, figuring the longer I could put off getting there, the better I would be. As I got closer to Fireman's Park, though, I blinked hard to capture what I was seeing. I knew a lot of people and media would show up, but I had no idea it would be this crazy. Cars and police were everywhere. Our little town of Brenham was in a full-swing traffic jam. People were parking wherever they could find a spot—even if their cars didn't fit the space. I maneuvered around some cars trying to squeeze in between cars already parked, and made it to the park's parking lot. A long rope hung across the entrance and a deputy sheriff stood guard. I had never seen anything like this before.

I pulled up to the rope and nodded to the deputy. He looked in the car and when he saw my green Cubs uniform, he walked over to the rope and lowered it so I could drive through. I pulled into one of the spots and parked.

Fireman's Park was nestled just off a main two-way street. Covered by a metal roof, wood bleachers wrapped around from the first to third base dugouts. Directly above the home plate seating area was the press box that housed the public address announcer, scorekeeper, and the local radio station sportscaster. The concession stand, restrooms, and ticket entrance were located behind the home plate seating area. Professional-style dugouts designed of cinder blocks that were painted Cub green were equipped with handcrafted wood benches, helmet and bat racks, and Astroturf. Freshly-manicured Tifway Bermuda grass covered the playing surface with the infield dirt being the right combination of clay and sand. Outlining the outfield area was a wooden fence with advertisements of local businesses. Directly above and behind the third base dugout on a hill some one hundred feet beyond was a train track operated by Union Pacific. Several times a game, trains traveled by, allegedly creating a "rally killer" for the opposing team. Fireman's Park was arguably one of the best high school baseball stadiums in the country, if not *the* best. And it was about to be the site where I would attempt to do something no one had done before.

Local and national media personnel had staged their areas by setting up their vans and antennas to broadcast the game live or provide updates to viewers periodically. Affiliates of ESPN, NBC, CBS, and ABC were all there. Instead of one concession stand, several others had been set up in antic- ipation of the large crowd. Law enforcement was stationed at every entrance to direct and control the mass of people. A makeshift seating area had been erected using an extended forklift with plywood as the floor and portable, fold-up chairs for viewing the game behind the right field fence. Hours before the game some fans had reserved their own seating by taping sheets of paper with their names on chairs behind the home plate fence area.

I grabbed my bag filled with my glove and cleats and briskly walked into the stadium with my hat pulled down low in hopes no one would corner me. I was not in the mood to answer questions or give people my fake smile that I was good at putting on.

But I also knew it was time to put aside the personal stuff and focus on the game. This was what I had worked so hard for, and now that I was here, I wanted this record. I needed to get laser-focused on the task at hand—to set the record straight once and for all.

Pregame activities began with our usual jog around the field followed by a series of warm-up routines in left field. While our team was stretching and getting warmed-up, the guys kept talking about the game and crowd.

"Pete, look at all these folks here. This is crazy," one of my teammates said.

Following our warm-up routine, we headed to pregame batting practice to the tune of the "ballpark music" playing in the background over the stadium speakers. We teed off with impressive shots spread all over the field. It was a time to get the juices flowing physically as well as mentally.

The team to beat was A&M Consolidated, a fierce district rival from College Station, forty-five minutes up the road from us.

They took the field for their pregame warm-up after we were finished. There was an unspoken, mutual respect for each other but when game time came around, we wanted to beat them as much as they wanted to beat us. And they didn't care they were the sacrificial offering this time around. They were going to make it tough for me to have an easy win.

As I watched their team warm up, I knew I needed to focus on their hitters' swings and find their weaknesses. But today was proving to be challenging. As much as I tried to keep focused on the game, the pain was not going away. It kept coming back as I thought about what had happened with Jill, wishing it were not true.

I made my way down the left field line to our bull pen to stretch and do some running prior to beginning my warm-up throws. Usually within the first couple tosses to the catcher, I could tell how the night on the mound was going to go. My arm either felt fresh and alive or dead. What made it feel one way or the other was a mystery to me, but on this night I quickly knew I would bring my best. With each warm-up throw I made, the less noise I heard in the background. My mind became crystal-clear. Baseball was my life, my future, and nothing was going to interfere with making my dream come true.

Walking to the dugout to wait for the starting lineup announcement and the National Anthem, I met our coach halfway. From the look on his face and his body expression, I knew he had something important to say. We walked together for several steps and stopped. He placed his hand on my shoulder and squeezed gently. "You've had a rough day. I don't know exactly what has happened but tonight is an opportunity of a lifetime. Put whatever it is out of your mind and just go for it."

"Yes, sir." I couldn't explain it, but the simple reassurance that he was on my side and was rooting for me was exactly what I needed to hear. It was as if he had lifted a weight off my shoulders and gave me a new sense of freedom. I think he knew that. It was now time to make it happen.

The pregame festivities were over. Someone had even found the previous record holder, Timmy Moore, of South Carolina, and flown him here to be present for the event and to throw out the first pitch. It all seemed surreal.

I stepped onto the mound as I had done dozens of times prior. And as usual, I felt the nervousness of butterflies in my stomach.

"Breeze it by him, Jon. Breeze it by him!" I recognized Mrs. Maass' high-pitched voice. She was my classmate Tadd Maass' mom. She always said the same thing, and I always liked catching her voice in the midst of the din.

I stared into the stands, overwhelmed at the number of people who had packed like sardines into the stadium. The majority was wearing green and white. In the middle behind home plate was my family. And there to my right and in the midst of the crowd, I spotted Jill. She was standing up, clapping and cheering me on with that smile I had fallen in love with. I did not know how it was going to turn out, but for the first time that day, I was glad to be living. I had been given a reprieve from what was really going on inside me and now I was experiencing the fun that came with the opportunity of a lifetime. Or perhaps it was a wink from above as to how life really should be. Whatever it was, I did not question it.

After one inning, the score was 3-0 in our favor and three strikeouts for A&M Consolidated. The more innings that passed by, the more our lead increased and the more batters I struck out. This thrill ride had entertained the audience for years. With each strike, the crowd grew louder. Was this going to be a night when not only the record books would be rewritten but the sentence would end with an exclamation mark—a no-hitter? I shivered with excitement.

Leading 8-0 and going into the bottom of the fifth inning, the fans edged forward on their seats and the media crept closer to the action. With such a large lead, the probability was high that this was to be the last inning. The ten-run rule was in effect, and if we scored two more runs, the game was over.

After a few hits and one of my teammates scoring a run, the scoreboard read 9-0 with only one out. The game-ending run was at second base with the meat of the batting order at the plate. And how fitting it was that I stood at the on-deck circle with a front-row view of the potential final score. One hit was all we needed to score one game-ending run.

Arguably one of our best hitters and the best pitcher on our team stood in the right-handed batter's box: James Nix. James and I had played baseball together since we were eight years old. He had become a good friend and was a huge part of our team's success. When I was not pitching, he was on the mound. He had racked up an impressive win-loss record that included only one loss, his first varsity outing. I often thought he did not get the recognition he deserved and because of the national record attention, he played second fiddle to me. It was not fair, in my opinion, but he never complained and instead worked as hard as anyone else. We fed off each other and made a great pitching battery—one of the best.

"End this thing right now!" I shouted from the on-deck circle as James stepped out of the batter's box and looked at me. He smiled and nodded.

But after swinging and missing three times, James walked past me and back to the dugout. "It's yours, Pete. Go for it."

Whatever battles had been going on, in and around me, vanished. The hurt, pain, and worries that had consumed me all day were gone as I stepped into the batter's box and stared down the opposing pitcher.

As the pitcher released the ball and it sped my way, I swung with all my might. Driving the ball to right field and running to first base, I turned my eyes toward home plate to watch my teammate easily score. Game over: 10-0.

The media rushed onto the field like a herd of bulls. My teammates stormed toward me like a pack of wild dogs and piled on me right there at first base. The flash of cameras was lighting up the sky. The crowd stood in amazement, clapping their hands and stomping their feet like they had just won the jackpot. The constant ringing in my ears I'd experienced all day was now joined by the chaotic sounds of celebration around me. And in the midst of all the commotion, time stopped for me. I was finally the United States national record holder for most consecutive wins in high school baseball at fifty-one wins and zero losses.

I was glad I hadn't missed it. I looked up into the stands and there was Jill, smiling, happy. And all the time, she had been there for me.

Left: At twenty weeks old, with my brother, Ronnie.
Right: Almost six years old. I already loved baseball.

My first Pee Wee Little League season.
At eight years old, I could finally play on a team.

In 1982, I played for the Indians Little League team
with my dad as the coach.
I'm on the back row, second from right. Even at eleven years old,
my size and uniform were different from everybody else's.

With Neal Pieper, my catcher.
I was a good foot taller than most of the kids.

Pitched a perfect game against Giddings in Navasota, Texas,
on July 14, 1983.
I struck out eighteen of eighteen and hit three homeruns.
This game received national attention, which surprised me since
I was only twelve.

Junior Little League World Series in Taylor, Michigan, Summer 1984.
We finished third in the world.

Posing with my mentor, Coach Lee Driggers, for the official varsity
baseball photos in Spring 1987, when I was a sophomore.
(Photo courtesy of James Luhn)

My hero and friend Jeff Toll, rubbing baseballs before a Class 4A
State Tournament game in June 1988.
(Photo courtesy of James Luhn)

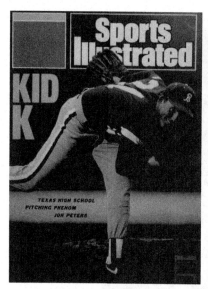

Left: The *Sports Illustrated* cover that was scheduled to run on May 9, 1988. Right: Pete Rose bumped an umpire, bumping me off the cover. (Copyright © Getty Images, Inc. Used by permission. All rights reserved.)

Just a portion of the overwhelming crowd at Fireman's Park in Brenham, Texas, ready to cheer me on during the record-breaking game in April 1989. (Photo courtesy of James Luhn)

Media frenzy after I broke the national record against the A&M Consolidated Tigers.
(Photo courtesy of James Luhn)

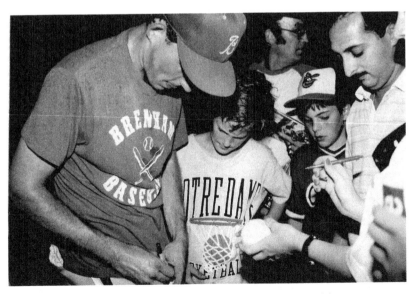
Signing autographs for fans after the record-breaking game.
(Photo courtesy of James Luhn)

Two pitchers posing. James Nix (left) and I took turns pitching.
He went on to sign with the Cincinnati Reds.
(Photo courtesy of James Luhn)

A family celebration. Mom and Dad came to all my games.
Ronnie (far right) flew in especially for the record-breaking game.
(Photo courtesy of James Luhn)

Enjoying the win with Coach Earl Hathaway after the
record-breaking game.
(Photo courtesy of James Luhn)

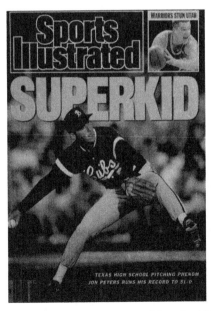

I finally made the cover on May 8, 1989!

Laughing and playing around with Jake and Kylie
during a local baseball game.

Sharing my story with the students
at Brenham High School in 2017.

CHAPTER 13
FINALLY FITTING IN

If I thought breaking the record the first time brought on a media circus, I had no idea what I was in for after I really broke the record. Every news outlet I could imagine wanted to talk with me. I finally made the cover of *Sports Illustrated*. I was on *The Today Show* and in *People* magazine, to name a very few. I received a personal note of congratulations from Nolan Ryan, and the Texas State Senate even congratulated me. I was named MVP and Player of the Year by multiple media outlets. One newspaper ran an article with a photo and the headline that read: "Is Perfection Enough?" It was all overwhelming. The one bright spot was that Jill and I were back together.

When the winning streak finally ended during game fifty-four against the West Orange-Stark Mustangs of Orange, Texas, not far from the Texas/Louisiana border, and I finished my high school career with fifty-three wins in a row, I was relieved the hype would finally be over. We went to State again, but lost in the semifinals. Oddly enough, I was okay with that too. I wanted a respite from the media—even though I knew they had turned their focus on what college I would attend and my upcoming college career. Everyone expected great things from me.

I had always wanted to go to The University of Texas because their baseball program was second to none. They constantly churned out pro ball players, whom I idolized: Bill Bates, Dennis Cook, Calvin Schiraldi, Roger Clemens, and Greg Swindell. I loved UT, because they always won. I also liked their coach, Cliff Gustafson. I liked his laid-back demeanor and how nothing ever seemed to phase him. From as far back as I can remember, I put on my UT hat and shirt, and then Dad and I would drive an hour and a half from Brenham to Austin—with me talking baseball the whole way, to watch UT play. At the ballpark, I joined all the other UT fans and clapped and chanted and raised my "hook 'em" sign with my right hand. I loved it and never wanted it to end.

Whenever I thought about attending college, I saw myself at UT. They would help me further my dreams and prepare me for the big leagues. I had spoken to Coach Gustafson previously and he knew UT was the school for me, that I lived it and breathed it. So when it came time to visit the UT campus and talk more in-depth with Coach Gustafson, I was excited—until I got there. My insecurities went into over-drive and I felt intimidated.

Who am I kidding? I thought. *I'm not good enough to be here.* I was sure as I was standing on the campus that if I went there, I would fail. To make matters worse, eight or nine other recruits were there. They looked and sounded impressive. *I can't go to this school and have them find out I'm not as talented as these guys, or as good as the coach thinks.*

Coach Gustafson spoke personally in his office with all the recruits and their families—except he didn't speak with me and my family personally in his office. That hurt my feelings.

When we were leaving, Coach smiled brightly at me and said, "Still coming to UT, Jon?"

Now was my chance to back out, not show my insecurities, and save what I saw as my dignity. "I'm not sure," I said, walking away from him, and I kept on walking. This was my excuse to make sure he never saw what a fraud I believed myself to be.

A few days later he called and asked what that was all about.

"Coach, you made time for everyone else, but not for me and my family."

His voice sounded surprised when he said, "I'm sorry, Jon. You have always said you wanted to play for The University of Texas and I figured you were 100 percent coming here."

"Well, I'm not sure now."

"Jon, are you sure about that? We'd love to have you on our team." He was going out of his way to offer me an opportunity to play at UT, but I just couldn't overcome my fear. I wished I'd felt more secure in who I was. If I did, I knew I would have signed immediately with UT and never looked back.

Instead, I chose Texas A&M University. A&M was another great school with a solid baseball program. I liked the school's laidback atmosphere, I already knew some of the guys on their team, and I liked that the school was so close to home, my friends, and Jill.

I graduated from high school, and that summer I played in the Karl Young League. My performance was sub-par but somehow, I made the All-Star team. During a game in Waco, at Baylor University, I was pitching when I noticed a twinge in my elbow when I extended it.

It's probably just overuse or I'm tired, I thought and didn't think much more about it.

I finished playing with them and took a break before starting college. Over the next few weeks of rest, I didn't notice any more trouble with my arm, so I figured it was just some freak thing that happened, but nothing I should be concerned about.

Then I got to A&M.

We started practicing in the fall for the spring season. The coaches use that semester to determine the strongest players and who will hold what position. I wanted to be a starter—even though I knew that would be tough to manage since I was only a freshman.

The first day of practice in September, I headed to our clubhouse to change into my practice uniform. I knew it wasn't fair to compare A&M's facilities to UT's but I was pleased to find that A&M's were just as nice, if not more. The stadium and facilities were top-notch. The clubhouse was like professional clubhouses. We had our own spacious lockers, practice and game uniforms were hung up for us, and we left all of our baseball stuff, like gloves, bats, and cleats there. It was first-class, and somehow it made me feel intimidated.

Then I walked down the tunnel from the clubhouse to the third base dugout and onto the field. I looked over at the bull pen, and there was a guy throwing there. He looked good.

What am I doing here? I'm not that good. I can't compete with that. It seemed like he was throwing so hard. Even with all the success I'd had, I still felt inferior, as though I didn't fit in.

I walked to the bull pen, where I met the catcher who was going to practice with me. He seemed like a good guy. But still I felt timid, not wanting to make a mistake, and wanting to get a lay of the land here. I was uncomfortable and anxious, not knowing what to expect. Would I be good enough to pitch for them?

With each pitch, my arm felt really strong. By practice's end, everybody told me what a great job I had done.

On the second day, we were doing "long toss," where I threw with a partner and as I got loose, the distance between my partner and me increased. One guy just keeps backing up. It develops arm strength. I noticed my arm was not as strong that day. That was not out of the norm since I had thrown in the bull pen the day before. But what I did notice was when I extended my arm to release the ball, a sharp twinge occurred. It was similar to hitting my funny bone. And the more I threw, the more painful it became.

At first I tried to cover it up. *It's just tired from yesterday,* I told myself, since I hadn't pitched in about two weeks before the previous day's practice. With each extension on every throw, though, it went from a twinge to a full-scale explosion, as though I had slammed my elbow against the edge of a table.

My mind slid back to passing out during the Junior Olympics because I had refused to tell anyone what was going on with my shoulder. I didn't want a repeat of that, so I strode over to the trainer, Mike Ricke. "Something isn't right in my elbow," I told him. I pointed to the spot that was giving me trouble.

He looked it over. As he stretched out my arm fully, I felt that sharp pain come again.

"There it is. Right where your left thumb is," I whined and grimaced. This wasn't just an elbow being worn out from a two-week vacation.

"Okay," Mike told me. "Take a break the rest of the day. Let me talk to Coach and I'll get back to you tomorrow."

This is bad, I thought, remembering getting on a plane and flying home from North Carolina. I didn't want to lose this opportunity to play college ball. But another part of my brain told me that whatever was going on, they'd fix it up and I'd be back and ready to go in no time.

I babied my elbow the rest of the night, fully anticipating that it would be okay the next day.

It wasn't. I returned to practice with the same painful extension. *This is just great. Arm pain on the second day of practice. I might as well just give up.*

"We're going to send you to Louisiana to see Dr. William Bundrick, an orthopedic surgeon who specializes in elbows," Mike told me. He had spoken with the coach and they felt this was the best option.

They made an appointment for me, and within a few days, my dad and I drove to Bossier City, Louisiana, a suburb of Shreveport, about four hours from the university. We pulled in at the Bone & Joint Clinic and met with Dr. Bundrick. He had graying hair and wore glasses, and he seemed very professional and serious.

After physically examining me and ordering tests, including an arthrogram—sticking a needle into my joint and injecting dye—he told me, "We found the problem. You have an abnormal bone growth on your elbow. When you fully extend your arm, bone is hitting bone. We will have to go in and shave part of your elbow, the bone, down. It's a very simple procedure."

I breathed a sigh of relief. *Okay, this is typical. Nothing major. Nothing to worry about. I can go in, get it done, and be back at practice by the spring.* "When can we get it taken care of?" I asked.

"I won't do the procedure," Dr. Bundrick said. "I'm going to refer you to Dr. James Andrews. He's in Birmingham, Alabama."

Alabama? Seriously? "Well, when can I get this done?"

"I'll contact him, and we'll see if he can fit you in quickly. Trust me, Dr. Andrews is very good at what he does."

Back at A&M, I learned that Dr. Andrews was "the man, the orthopedic guru." And within seven to ten days, my mother and I were sitting in his office at the Andrews Sports Medicine and Orthopaedic Center where they do surgery and all kinds of sports' medical research. I liked him immediately. He was not a man for small-talk, and seemed competent and confident. I also knew he had worked on several real big-time guys, like Bo Jackson, one of the few athletes named All-Star in both professional baseball and football.

He looked at my X-rays, confirmed Dr. Bundrick's diagnosis, and scheduled the surgery for the following day.

"This is really not a big deal," he told me. "However, it's going to be very painful."

"What's so painful?" I asked.

"Any time we deal with bone, it's painful. However, it's a very easy procedure where we will go in arthroscopically, and make a few tiny incisions."

"I've been having trouble straightening my arm fully. Will this surgery help that as well?"

"No . . ." He paused for a moment, thinking. "While I'm shaving the bone down, I'll look at what's going on and will try to straighten your arm. Since we're doing surgery any way, if I break the bone, we can always fix it."

I wasn't sure how I felt about that! But I figured he knew what he was doing, so I just nodded and said okay.

Then he smiled. "You'll recover from this injury. No problem."

Well, he was right about at least one thing. After I came out of surgery, any movement of my arm felt excruciating. I sure wasn't going to take *Tylenol* to alleviate any of the pain, remembering my last experience with that drug!

While I was in recovery, Dr. Andrews came in and told me that everything had gone well. The only problem was that he had been unable to straighten my arm fully. So in addition to rehab, he ordered me in an arm brace that could be tightened to help straighten my arm. It was like a knee brace with a wrap around my upper arm and a wrap around my forearm and with two metal pins on the outside of my elbow. He explained it was like the theory of straightening a tree. It had to be done consistently. It looked scary, but he felt it would work, so I was all in.

Once I was back home, I began rehab. The training staff, mainly Mike, had me on a strict schedule. For eight weeks, every Monday through Friday after my college classes, I worked on stretching and strengthening my arm with the goal of getting it ready for the spring season.

I also wore the arm straightening brace every day for one to two hours at a time. I couldn't wear it longer than that because my arm would get too sore. As my arm slowly straightened, we would tighten the brace. However, my arm never would fully straighten.

One afternoon in October, not long after my surgery, the coach, Mark Johnson, called me to his office. "Jon, I've talked with the other coaches and we'd like to see you fully recover from your arm injury and not rush you back," he said. "We are going to redshirt you this year so you can focus on rehab and coming back strong for next fall."

I breathed a sigh of relief. This was the best thing he could have told me. In college sports, an athlete has four years of eligibility. If a coach redshirts a player, that means that after his freshman year, the player would still have four years of eligibility. If they didn't redshirt me that year, even if I didn't play, that year would have been used for my eligibility. So then after my freshman year, I'd have only three years of eligibility left.

"Thanks, Coach. I appreciate that."

I meant that, but I still missed playing ball and being more of a team player. Through the remainder of the fall season, as I worked 100 percent in rehab, I watched my teammates, whom I barely knew, go on with their college ball careers, while mine was stuck. I *wanted* to play; I *wanted* to really be part of the team. I *wanted* to feel as if I belonged—and that became a recipe for disaster.

"The guys are heading out tonight," said my roommate, Brian, who was also on the team as an outfielder. "Want to join us?"

Some of my teammates hit the local bars every weekend to drink and party. Since I had never been much of a partier—even in high school I didn't drink—I had always passed whenever invited. But now week after week went by as I watched the others practice while I faithfully went to rehab. I missed playing baseball. I missed the team camaraderie.

"Yeah, cool. I'll go," I said, to my roommate's surprise.

I had no idea how we were going to get into a bar or order a drink, since we were both just nineteen and the legal drinking age was twenty-one, but I figured I'd just go along for the sober fun and maybe play some pool.

I found a table and sat, while my friends grabbed beers from the bar. They came back carrying two pitchers of beer and mugs. "Here you go. Drink up. This will make you forget all your troubles with that elbow!"

"How did you get these?" I asked, dumbfounded.

They looked over at some of the upperclassmen and winked at me. Those guys were all over twenty-one. They could legally buy drinks.

I took the mug, filled it with beer, and looked down at it. *No big deal*, I told myself. *It's just one drink. Everyone is doing it.* I hoped this would be the ticket to helping me bond with my teammates, to be accepted and just one of the guys. I took a sip and coughed a little at its strong flavor. It felt warm going down my throat. And soon, sip after sip, I felt myself become peaceful, more calm and confident. I felt free and happy!

"Here, try this," one of my friends who had come with us said, as he put a different drink on our table.

"What is it?" I asked.

"Mumbo-jumbo," he said. "Limeade and a whole lot of gin." He laughed.

If beer made me feel this good, I figured the mumbo-jumbo would do the same. I was wrong. It was even better!

I took a sip and was hooked. "Man, this is awesome!" I shouted. I was loud and proud.

"I know, right?" he said, taking another sip.

No more insecurities. Only confidence. I finally fit in. I could say anything I wanted. I could do whatever I wanted. Then I vomited.

It's funny how quickly the mind can forget awful things. By the next weekend, I had forgotten the vomiting and just remembered how good drinking made me feel. So when the next invitation came to join the guys at a local bar, I was all in!

I wasn't interested in just drinking. I wanted to get drunk. The sips were replaced with gulps.

The cycle was always the same: a round of mumbo-jumbos, an increased feeling that I belonged, that I was a-okay, and then I'd throw up. By Saturday morning, I was a mess, but after a jog and by that evening, I felt pretty good and was set to do it all again. And no drinking with food. Why eat? If I ate, I couldn't drink as much.

After a while I figured, why go *out* to drink? I had one of our older teammates pick up some gin for me, and on Fridays after class and our team workouts, I would head back to the dorm room, take an old milk carton, and make my own concoction of mumbo-jumbo. A hint of limeade; a whole lot of gin. And no sipping! I chugged it down all the way. And all my problems disappeared—my problems with baseball, with school work, with relationships.

As so many high school couples do when distance separates them, Jill and I felt that distance and broke up. And I knew this time, it was for good. I had hurt her too much, we were arguing too often, and I was trying to find my way in a new place and not doing that very well. I ached over this loss. But with my new friend, alcohol, that was okay. I would get through it.

My school work suffered and my math scores were so low that I had to drop the class or fail it (a terrible thing, given my dad was a math professor), but with my new friend, alcohol, that was okay too.

My elbow wasn't quite coming back the way it should have. And even that was okay, because my friend, alcohol, was helping me manage. Alcohol never judged me, never thought I wasn't good enough. Alcohol accepted me just as I was and made me feel the best I had ever felt in my life. It filled that hole in my soul I had.

Sure, I still vomited every time. But it was worth the price because of how wonderful it made me feel. I felt so good, in fact, that I knew there was nothing I couldn't do—including drive.

Several times I would get smashed and then head to Brenham to watch the high school football team play. It always felt like I could drive better when I was drunk.

During one such trip, a friend and I packed a cooler with beer and drank the whole way to the football game, which was an away game somewhere just outside of Houston. When I was finished with one beer, Mark would reach into the cooler and get me a replacement. We drank there, we drank during the game, and then we drank on the drive back to College Station. The drive seemed way too long to go the speed limit, so I pushed the accelerator down to the floor and flew down the road.

"Uh, hey, Jon," Mark said. "Was that a cop you just passed?"

I looked in my rearview mirror. A state trooper's car was turning around and coming up behind us with his blue and red lights whirling.

Mark reached into his pocket and pulled out a packet of gum. "Here," he said, putting an unwrapped stick into my hand. "Chew this."

As soon as the cop car caught up with us, he blared his siren, indicating that I should pull over.

"Aw, man," I said, adding a few other choice words and sobering up quickly. I was busted this time. I was probably going to lose my license and go to jail.

Through my side mirror, I watched the trooper get out of his car and walk up to mine. I chewed my gum faster.

"Driver's license and registration, please," he said.

Mark already had both out ready for me to hand to the officer.

The trooper looked at them and then back at me. "Where are you going so fast?"

"Going back to A&M, sir," I said, as calmly and undrunk as I could.

"You were going eight-six miles an hour. I'll be right back." He took my information with him back to his car, while I waited, trying to figure out how I was going to explain to my parents that I was busted for DUI.

Within a few minutes, the officer was back at my window, handing me my license and registration. "You the pitcher?" he asked.

I was surprised by the question. "Yes, sir," I said simply.

"Okay. Slow it down and have a safe trip." He knocked on the side of the car, turned, and headed back to his vehicle.

I might not have liked the media attention to my baseball skills, but I certainly didn't mind this aspect of the fame!

The spring slowly came and I continued to party and go to classes. I was determined to get my arm back. I doubled up on my rehab and strengthening exercises, my jogging, and even my classwork. The partying didn't affect those things, I knew, so there was no reason to curtail them. After all, I needed *some* release from all the stress.

It didn't matter that my release was bigger, louder, more boisterous, and more destructive than anybody else's. I became the life of the party. I might not be able to shine out on the field that season, but I was a winner at the after parties!

By the fall of 1990, I entered my sophomore year raring and ready to go. My arm felt great and I held my own during the fall practice season. But after the six weeks of hard practice, Coach Johnson had me rated as the number seven pitcher.

"Number seven?" I said out loud, after seeing the pitching lineup. I had performed better than a number seven spot. I looked at the rest of the pitchers and their status. I saw the names of a couple of the guys ahead of me. *Ah, no, no, no. No! I outperformed them. No, this is* not *right.* In my gut, even a number seven spot would have ensured some solid playing time, but my head didn't want to hear of it. I'd been gypped. And I was not about to stand for that.

I would go somewhere where they appreciated my abilities, where they would let me be a starter, a number one, not a number seven.

I knew Coach Van Hook and Coach McElreath at Blinn College, a junior college in Brenham, where my dad taught math, so I called them.

"I'm just wondering what your pitching needs are for this season?"

Coach McElreath paused, I'm guessing because I shocked him with the question. "Jon, if you come here, you will *definitely* be one of our starters."

Music to my ears. I thought it would be better to go to Blinn because I would be able to pitch a lot more. Even at a junior college, I figured pro ball scouts would be more impressed that I was able to pitch than never get to see me pitch because I was so far down on the pitching roster, the scouts would be gone by the time the game got to me.

The next week I walked into Coach Johnson's office and announced I was leaving A&M, that this semester would be my last. I knew that meant I would never have an opportunity to play an actual game at the school, but so be it. "I'm transferring to Blinn where I'll get more playing time and be able to get back in shape and use my arm more."

He grimaced and shook his head, clearly not liking my news. "I don't agree with this decision, Jon. I don't think you need to go to Blinn. I think you need to stay here and use this next year as a year to get back into it. You're *going* to get a chance to play."

I didn't believe him, and I had made up my mind.

"You know if you leave A&M, your scholarship will be gone. And there's no guarantee that you'll be able to return here and play ball."

"I understand," I said, not thinking that would be a problem. I'd play at junior college, get my arm back in shape, return to A&M, show them all I had what it took to be a starter for them, and everything would be set. But there was no way I was staying and not getting to be a starter.

It was settled. It was time for me to fall back on my MO and run away again.

CHAPTER 14
MORE TROUBLE

"Peters decides to leave A&M," the *Lubbock Avalanche Journal* of West Texas announced. Nobody gets written up because they transfer to a different school, but I did. Papers from all over the state were interested that I was leaving A&M and going to Blinn College, back home in Brenham, to join forces with the blue and white Blinn Buccaneers.

I was excited to go back to everything familiar. I would live at home, get to play as a starting pitcher, and reconnect with my high school friends—although my relationship with Jill was not meant to be, and she was now seeing someone else.

I started the spring 1991 season with a new team—several of them I had played with on our high school team—and a new lease on my dreams. I practiced hard, determined to show everyone I had made the right decision. We had a good team and a lot of good pitchers who could have been playing at Division I baseball programs, but for one reason or another chose to play junior college ball. Usually it was because of grades but for some, it was finances or to develop their skills further.

Our first game was coming up and I had to show everybody I still had the goods. We practiced long and hard and our team was ready to face our opponent, San Jacinto College. They had won numerous national titles, and they were in our conference. I was the starting pitcher and was doing well. After five innings we were winning and I was still pitching, but I was getting tired.

"How you holding up?" Coach Van Hook asked me after the fifth inning.

"Good. The arm feels good," I told him.

"Not getting tired?"

"No, sir. I'm good."

By the sixth inning, we were losing. Coach knew I had not been straight up with him. Batter after batter was getting past me. Hit after hit came fast and furious, and Coach Van Hook finally stepped out of the dugout and walked toward the mound. My heart sank.

"You gave it your best," he told me on the mound, surrounded by the catcher and several of the infielders. I cringed as I handed over the ball, he patted me on the backside, and they all watched me walk from the mound, feeling disgraced.

Changing pitchers happens all the time. It's normal for any game. But it didn't happen when *I* was on the mound. This was an atypical experience, and I didn't like it.

I ended up losing that game for my team. And I didn't think I could feel worse than being pulled. I discovered at the end of the game, that yes, I could.

A couple days later the weather was misting and in the forties. Because it had rained earlier, we could not practice on the field. Outside the locker room and directly across the parking lot from the stadium was a wide open field that the school used for such activities as intramural football and band practice. The pitchers and catchers went there to throw and afterwards to condition or run. Basically we did a mini version of long toss, just to do something and to get the blood flowing. I was playing catch with Craig Bolcerek, our catcher.

My elbow felt sore and I was hoping it would loosen up during our stretching exercises before we played catch. It was usually sore for a few days after I pitched a game, but this soreness was different, abnormal.

Man, this doesn't feel good.

It was very tight, like rubber bands were inside and about to pop. I tried to dismiss it and did not say anything about it. As we began throwing, however, I knew something was not right. I had never felt anything like it before. In addition to being very tight, it was very weak. I had to really focus on where I was throwing the ball because my arm wasn't working properly, as though something was disrupting the message from my brain to my arm and delaying my arm from working the way it should.

With each throw, my elbow kept locking up. No matter what stretches I tried, I could not get my arm loose. I would try to throw, but every motion hurt. A panicked, sick feeling grew in my gut. *Oh my goodness, what is this?* But I didn't say anything, determined to tough it out.

Instead I just told Craig that I was loose and I'd had enough.

The next game I was scheduled to pitch was eight days later. We were facing Angelina College at their home in Lufkin, Texas. But my arm still wasn't right. Every pitch brought a lock, a click, and a twinge in my elbow, along with a numbness emitting from the elbow and going down to my fingertips. I was barely throwing eighty-mile-an-hour balls, if that. But surprisingly, we won. I was never so glad to finish a game. By the end I could barely pick up and grasp a ball without pain. I could no longer ignore what was happening to my arm.

I still wasn't ready to admit there was a problem, though, so I decided to focus on resting it as much as I could. At A&M, I would have just drunk my troubles away, but living at home meant I had to curtail the drinking, and I was okay with that, for the most part. Every once in a while I headed out to the bars to meet up with some friends and get drunk. The worst was at an away game, though, in early March. We traveled down to the border town of Brownsville, Texas, to play a three-game conference series against Texas Southmost College, two games on Saturday and one on Sunday. I wasn't scheduled to start any of the games because I had shared earlier with the coach that my elbow had been feeling sore. He told me that if I started to feel better, he would possibly use me as a relief pitcher, if he needed to. Texas Southmost was not that good compared to our team so I really never expected to be used during any of the games.

After we won the two games on Saturday, we all went back to our hotel and received meal money to use however we wanted. There were restaurants within walking distance, so my roommate and I headed over to one of the national chains we liked. It felt good to be able to order a drink and be legal about it, now that I was twenty-one! We ordered a drink that consisted of some concoction of fruit juices and rum.

We kept ordering as fast as the server could bring them. We figured it wasn't a problem, since we could walk back to our hotel room. But eventually my roommate said, "We've got that game tomorrow. Maybe we should slow it down."

"Nah," I told him. "We're good!" It didn't matter what was happening the next day, I had my partying on and I was feeling fine.

It was late when we finally left the restaurant and I had to use the restroom. Rather than go back inside the restaurant, though, I decided to hop on top of a car in the parking lot and urinate on the hood. Seemed like a good and funny idea. Then we went back to our room, where I laid down. As soon as my head hit the pillow, though, the room started spinning and once again, I started to vomit. Into the early morning hours I vomited, and then when I had nothing left to bring up, I dry heaved. I felt awful and could only moan between my "episodes."

The next day I was scheduled to relief pitch, if the coach needed me in the game, but I was too hungover, dehydrated, exhausted, and headachy. I did my best to warm up with the team and I threw some tosses to play catch, but I had no intention of pitching that day. All I wanted was to lie down in a cold, dark room and force my head to quit pulsating with each heartbeat.

"Coach, I can't pitch today. My arm hurts too bad." That was the first time I had ever lied to a coach. Well, not truly lied—I'm sure my arm did hurt. It was just that my head hurt worse, but I couldn't tell *him* that. This was the first time I had not been able to play because of my drinking, and it was the first time that I really didn't *want* to play, which was unlike me. I always wanted to play! My guilt weighed heavily upon me.

Coach took me at my word and told me it was okay. They'd substitute another pitcher and I could rest.

Once I was back in my right mind, I realized how terrible what I had done was. So I committed to going all-out for the next game. At the next practice, I started pitching with my catcher in the bull pen and immediately the pain was back in my elbow, along with shooting arrows of numbness down to my fingertips.

There would be no way I would make it through the practice, let alone our upcoming game. I had already lost one game for Blinn. I wasn't about to do that again.

I turned toward Coach Van Hook, who was the pitching coach in addition to the head coach. "Something's going on with my elbow," I told him.

He shut me down from throwing right then. And back to Andrews Sports Medicine and Orthopaedic Center in Birmingham, Alabama, my mom and I went. On the short, two-hour flight there, I looked out the window without seeing anything of the beautiful landscape below. I had a terrible feeling about this injury, that it wasn't just a quick fix. This was serious, possibly dream crushing, I was sure of it.

As we made our descent to Birmingham, the smooth flight didn't match the turbulence in my spirit. I had not done anything wrong, but for no apparent reason, all my dreams were being taken away. Like a kite with its string cut, my dreams were drifting further from me, leaving me alone to mourn their loss. And I was terribly afraid.

The office staff and doctor were ready for our arrival, and immediately they began a battery of tests to determine the cause of my pain.

Dr. Andrews conducted a physical examination and talked with us for a while. I had gained a lot of trust and confidence in him from an earlier surgery, not to mention, his pioneering approaches to orthopedic medicine were advanced in know-how as well as technology. As he examined my elbow with a few simple twists and turns, it was apparent he had some idea of what was causing my issue. However, without having conclusive evidence, he refrained to suggest the possibilities and ordered further testing.

"Let's do another arthrogram—stick a needle in the joint and inject dye." I cringed at having it done again, but I knew our options were limited and that it was important. I sighed and nodded.

Afterward, we sat in one of the patient rooms and silently waited. Outside, the voices of doctors and nurses were muzzled and hard to understand. The opening and closing of doors and the footsteps outside the room echoed throughout the floor level. I was not in the mood to talk about anything, even though my unspoken words were saying so much.

The longer we waited, the more nervous I became. My heart had fallen into the pit of my stomach with a gnawing fear. It was not like butterflies fluttering or a churning feeling that I experienced before a big game, but an escalating, intense feeling of impending doom. I had worked myself into such a state that I felt ready to burst out crying.

After about an hour, the door opened and in stepped a resident. He was from my neck of the woods and had taken an interest in my case. He talked with us for a short time before he illuminated the arthrogram films. I had no idea what I was looking at, so my breath caught when he said, "Well, it doesn't appear you have any tears. It's probably tendonitis, but let's wait until Dr. Andrews comes in."

I'd had tendinitis in the past, and even though this felt different—more painful—I exhaled with relief.

"I don't know, this is probably a three-to-four-week deal and you'll be fine. It's normal for pitchers," he continued.

I wanted to jump from my seat, throw my arms around him, and give him a big hug! My face lit up and I felt free again. I joked and relaxed. I had fretted over nothing!

Andrews is going to come in here and say, "This is what you need to do. See you later. Get on the plane," I thought.

I looked at my mom and we smiled brightly at each other. "Sounds like I need to rest some and I will be back in a few weeks," I said. "We flew all the way up here for this news, but it was sure worth it." I wanted to jump up and down while pumping my fists. This was the best news I had heard in a while. *When will I learn to stop projecting the worst-case scenario onto everything and replace my negative thoughts with positive ones?* I wondered.

I now eagerly awaited Dr. Andrews' arrival, where I expected he'd talk with us a little and give me a detailed exercise program for the next four to six weeks to combat the inflammation. Then we'd be free to head back home. It would be a quick trip to hear little news but, to me, that was some of the greatest news to hear. My nerves had subsided. It was time to get out of the clinic—I'd had enough of this place.

About twenty or thirty minutes later, Dr. Andrews came in. He shook my hand and looked me in the eyes. "Let's take a look at the CAT scan and see what we have going on."

He turned on the viewing light to illuminate the film and immediately pointed to a spot. "Right there. Yep, right there you've got a pretty good tear."

I blinked. *Ah, what?*

"Yeah, you've got a big tear right here in your ulnar collateral ligament. It's going to require Tommy John surgery."

His words weren't sinking in. *A tear?* I thought, now feeling confused. *How is that possible? He didn't even hardly look and bam. I thought I had tendonitis and everything was fine. That was what the resident told me. If it's that clear to you, how did the resident miss it?*

Puzzled by the different opinions and dazed because of the pendulum swing of great news to terrible news, I was speechless. Even if I could say anything, what words were appropriate? My world had just flipped upside down and it had happened so fast. It suddenly became apparent that this was not going to be such a quick trip.

"What's Tommy John surgery?" my mother asked.

Dr. Andrews explained that Tommy John was a left-handed pitcher for the New York Yankees. He was the first pitcher who had this ulnar collateral ligament surgery performed. The procedure calls for the doctor to take either a tendon or a ligament from the person's wrist or ankle and transplant it.

So Dr. Andrews would graft each side of the tendon on either side of my elbow. He explained that he would take the ulnar nerve out and lay it on a plate. He would have to be careful not to touch the nerve much because that would damage the nerve endings. And then he would do the graft.

This sounded like a major and complex surgery. A transplant would not lend itself well to the quick fix I was hoping for.

"And the recovery time?" my mother asked.

"Typically we're looking at a six- to nine-month recovery period. That will include extensive rehabilitation with a slow, progressive throwing program." He turned his attention back to me. "Can you do this?" He took his middle finger and touched his thumb.

So I did what he asked with my right hand, and he rubbed my wrist until what looked like a vein popped out prominently.

"Okay, you have that tendon."

"What?"

"Some people don't have that tendon. You do, so that's good. We will take that out and graft it."

"What's the tendon used for?" I asked.

"I don't know."

"Did Tommy John go back to playing baseball after his surgery?" my mother asked.

"Yes," Dr. Andrews said. "But there are no guarantees. Some pitchers never fully recover from this surgery." He looked at me and smiled confidently. "Jon is young. He'll recover. We'll get it back to normal. Don't worry about it."

While I wasn't thrilled at the prospect of having a third surgery, I trusted Dr. Andrews and felt reassured that if he said I'd be back playing ball, then I would be back playing ball.

He scheduled me for surgery the next day, and Mom and I went to our hotel to wait.

Mom tried to comfort me, asking if I wanted to go out to eat or if she could get me anything or if I wanted to talk about anything, but I didn't want to talk and I didn't want her comfort.

"I'm going to call Dad and let him know," she told me.

"I don't want to talk to him," I said, bluntly.

As much as I wanted to believe Dr. Andrews' confident words, I kept replaying his other, more damning ones. *"Many players never recover . . . major surgery . . . end their careers . . ."*

What if he was wrong about my situation? I was not ready to give up, but all the signals indicated a fruitless and dooming return. Arm surgery did not bode well for a pitcher. But now three of them?

Lying on my stomach with a pillow under my chest, I gazed blankly at the television. *Is this it? Am I done? Now what do I do with the rest of my life?* This frustration and darkness had been building for hours, but so far, I had managed to stay strong without any bursts of anger or episodes of tears. It took everything in me to fake that I was okay and not bawl my eyes out. But I didn't want my mom to worry. More importantly, I did not want her to think I was weak. I was a man now. I should be able to face this with strength and dignity.

After a few hours of being cooped up inside the hotel room, I felt stir-crazy. The reality of the news was finally sinking in. Even though Dr. Andrews assured me that I would come through this fine and would play ball again, I knew deep down in my gut that I would not. The more I obsessed over the possibility of never pitching again, the more hollow and empty my heart felt. It was too early to call it a night, so I decided to take a walk around the nearby area and get some fresh air.

"I'm going out," I told my mom. "Be back in a bit."

"Okay, dear," she said simply. "Jon, if you give it to God, he'll help you through this."

I didn't answer her. I had prayed some before and God hadn't seemed to answer those prayers. I wasn't interested in giving him another try.

Isolation from anyone and everyone was my ammunition when I was in my world of self-pity. If I was alone, others were not able to ask me questions to find out what was really going on inside me. I did not want to hear any suggestions or comments—that was only fuel to start an argument. And usually, after I sulked in my sorrow for a while, I came back around. That's what I hoped for this time too.

Strolling aimlessly through the hotel's halls, I finally let my emotions carry me away and tears of fear and sadness rolled down my cheeks. Baseball was one of the few things I truly loved and I was terrified of losing it. It was the only place I felt I fit in. What would happen to me if I no longer had that?

And what would others say if I never played again? My identity had been tied so closely with my achievements in baseball that apart from it, I didn't know who I was. How would others view me? What would Coach Driggers think if he saw me now? Would he still like me? Would everybody be disappointed and feel I let them down? Would they call me names, believing I was a loser and a quitter? Or perhaps worse, would they talk about me in hushed tones as the boy who got so close and then choked?

And how was I going to do rehab this time around? I didn't have the A&M trainers. Blinn was a junior college; they didn't have funds or access to professional athletic trainers and rehabilitation equipment.

I made my way down to the hotel lobby and sat on a comfortable, cushioned chair far from the front desk and hidden near the pool entrance. It was a quiet evening with few guests checking in or walking about. The third surgery in the past four years did not lend itself well to attracting the attention of major-league scouts, and the probability of making it big was slim to none. *Who's going to draft a kid who's already had three surgeries—and this one major? Nobody.* And I knew the chances of another injury were high, especially with the bad mechanics I had developed after my first surgery. I sat quietly, allowing my mind to go wherever it wanted, which was down to the deepest, darkest depths. Slumped over with my elbows on my knees and my head resting in the palms of my hands, I began to bawl.

CHAPTER 15
COMING TO GRIPS

Surgery went well, according to Dr. Andrews. The night before surgery I was down in the dumps, but now I had work to do. No more pity parties. Three times a week for almost nine months, I drove to Bryan, forty-two miles from Brenham, to do my physical therapy workouts with Mike Joseph. Before he released me from the hospital, Dr. Andrews had warned me to make sure to strengthen my elbow the same as I strengthened my shoulder, because he didn't want my elbow to get strong at the expense of my shoulder getting weak. "Don't favor it," he said.

I tried not to, but that was difficult—especially because I had so much work to do on getting my elbow healed. Stretching my arm to full extension was hard but surprisingly not painful. What did hurt was when Mike pinched the stitched area. I had scar tissue that had built up along the eight-inch incision, so he would pinch it hard to crack it and break it up. That hurt worse than anything! But still I suffered through it and gave 100 percent during every therapy session, keeping focused on the goal: to pitch again.

By the second semester of my junior year, spring 1992, I was ready to play ball. The Blinn Buccaneers were starting practice, and I was excited to get back in the game with my teammates. It felt good to return to the bull pen with my catcher. I warmed up my arm, paying attention to my elbow. It felt good. I threw a few balls. Everything seemed okay, although I felt timid. My mind-set, something I could always control in the past, didn't want to cooperate with me now and I started to doubt my talents.

You can't throw with the same speed, my mind told me. *Your power is gone.*

I tried to ignore those pesky thoughts, but my body wasn't cooperating. My elbow seemed fine, but my right shoulder hurt. It seemed tender and weak, and when I moved it around, I could hear a slight crackling sound. *That's not good.* I exhaled disgustedly. *Here we go again.* I was angry with my body that it kept breaking down on me. I knew I couldn't fake it as I had tried so many times before, even though it killed me to admit it. With a heavy sigh I turned to Coach Van Hook, who was standing behind me. "Coach, it's my shoulder now. It hurts."

This time I scheduled an appointment with a doctor in College Station, Texas, by A&M. He had worked with Dr. Andrews so I knew I could trust him.

"You've got a tear in your rotator cuff," he told me, looking at my CAT scan results.

I racked my brain trying to come up with some memory of how I might have done this, but I could think of nothing. I knew I had developed bad pitching mechanics in which I threw with just my arm and not with my legs and whole body, like pitchers are supposed to. I knew I was dipping my back shoulder instead of keeping it straight. Was that what had caused it? But even with that, I couldn't remember any particular scene, no obvious wrong movement, no incorrect therapy exercise. Nothing.

"We can repair it arthroscopically and after some recovery time, you should be good to go," he said.

Why does this keep happening? I groaned inwardly and shook my head at him. No, I most definitely would not be good to go. Even if an MLB scout was willing to give me a chance with three surgeries, no one in his right mind would take a risk on a rookie pitcher who'd had four surgeries. It was time to face the truth: I was done.

I'm just a loser. Everything in my life had led me to one place: playing baseball. All my career preparation, my life's goals, my dreams—all baseball. All my hard work wasted. Now what was I supposed to do?

I'd been the best—I had the media coverage and the *Sports Illustrated* cover and the *Good Morning America* television appearance to prove it. And for what? I was now going to be the guy who once had been great; the kid who'd had such a promising future. I was going to be the *has been*, the *once was*, the *used to be*. I thought about my teammates who still had their futures to look forward to. What did I have? Nothing. Everybody had put me on a pedestal and soon the real Jon was going to come out. No longer was I going to be this topnotch baseball player. I was just going to be some normal guy who I didn't really know how to be. I didn't even have Jill. I had no girlfriend, no fallback plan, no outlook, no hope. A small part of my brain pushed me to have the surgery, to keep going, but I pushed it aside. I was tired and I knew the surgery might help my shoulder, but it wouldn't resuscitate my dreams.

"If I don't get it repaired will it be okay?" I just couldn't bring myself to suffering through yet another surgery—especially if I didn't have to.

"If you don't get it fixed now, you'll have worse trouble with it later in life."

I sighed heavily—something I felt as if I was doing a lot of lately. "Okay, let's do it." One more surgery, but this time not to make me better for baseball, but to ensure that I didn't have lasting effects decades later.

After I left his office I thought about driving straight to the closest bar and drinking myself into oblivion, but even that didn't hold any appeal to me. Instead I went home, climbed into bed, and cried myself to sleep.

A week after my surgery, I called Coach Johnson at A&M. Because Blinn was a junior college, it wouldn't provide me with a bachelor's degree, so I decided to return to A&M to finish my schooling. I knew I no longer had the baseball scholarship and I couldn't play ball, but I wondered if somehow I could still be involved with the team.

"Coach, is there any possibility I can be an undergraduate assistant coach?"

"As a matter of fact, the NCAA just came out with a rule that any former player can be an undergraduate assistant," Coach said. The NCAA is the National College Athletic Association and they make the rules on what can and can't go on in college sports. "Why don't you come over here and talk to me about it."

The next day I drove to College Station.

"Undergraduate assistant coach, huh?" he said. "So you're done playing?"

"Yes, sir. I tore my rotator cuff." I explained about my injuries and how I was tired of feeling as though I was always in rehab and how spending the majority of my time on the training table instead of the ball field had gotten old. "It just isn't fun anymore."

He nodded as though he understood. Then he offered me the position. And in the fall of 1992, I returned to A&M as a junior, since I didn't have enough credits to be a senior, even though it was my fourth year of school. But I didn't care; I felt excited again. I might not be on the mound, but I could throw batting practice and I could offer suggestions and insight as a coach. My god of baseball had come through for me again. I was part of the team, part of the game, without the rehab and the injuries—and the media attention.

That helped curtail most of my drinking, but not completely. Not long after the school year started, I attended a wedding in Industry, Texas, which is twenty minutes from Brenham, and I got drunk at the reception. On the drive home, I was on a road that had a dangerous curve at the bottom of a steep hill—so dangerous that I'd known people who had died on it. Beyond the curve was a fifteen to twenty foot drop into a pasture. Not far into the pasture was a giant oak tree, which several people had smacked into when their cars careened off the road.

As I approached that section of the road, I thought, *Okay, this is the turn. You got to slow down.* But my foot jammed down on the accelerator instead. As I sped into the curve, I lost control and went off the road. For some reason, I had the presence of mind to tell myself to relax. While the car flipped over, flew into a ditch, and landed in a pasture, I willed myself to stay calm.

It was pitch black out, so I couldn't see the damage or where I was, but I knew I needed to get up to the road to flag down a passing car. Soon one came, and a kind couple offered to drive me home.

"Goodness, what happened to you?" my mother asked as soon as I walked into the house.

I looked down at my suit coat and saw tiny pieces of glass all over it. "I had a wreck."

"Where?" my dad asked.

"Right on that turn."

"How'd you get home?" he said.

"Some couple picked me up and brought me."

"I'm on my way over there," he said and headed out of the house.

I didn't care where he was going. My face felt hot and my left eye hurt, so I was more interested to check on what damage I had done to myself. I walked to the bathroom and looked in the mirror. My eye was swollen shut and it felt like a bone just underneath it was broken. That sobered me up.

When my dad returned several hours later, he looked tired. "There were blue and red lights everywhere when I got out there," he said. "The police officer told me that if you have an accident again like that and you don't stay on site, he's going to arrest you for fleeing the scene of an accident, so next time you stay."

I nodded, but my head hurt.

"Also, they asked me if you were drinking, and I told them no. But when I walked around your car, there were a bunch of beer cans. When they weren't looking, I kicked them into the distance. I also told the officer you had your seatbelt on. Is that true?" Without waiting for me to answer, he continued.

"The officer said if you didn't have your seatbelt on, you would more than likely be dead."

"Well, I didn't have my seatbelt on."

Dad shook his head but said nothing more.

The next day Dad and I drove out to look at the car, which by now had been moved. There in the middle of the storage lot, sat my blue, four-door Honda Civic, barely recognizable. The roof was caved in, the windshield and back window were gone, glass was everywhere. This was some accident. And all I could remember of it was telling myself to relax.

By Monday morning I had another car and no consequences. And by the next weekend, when some of the team went out to the local bar, I was right there with them. I got drunk, vomited, and was ready to do it again the next weekend and the next. Even almost dying didn't give me pause or second thoughts about my unhealthy relationship with alcohol. It made me feel okay. When I was liquored up, I wasn't a has-been or a washed-up ball player. I wasn't just a "normal" guy. I was *somebody* again.

● ● ●

With the ability to help coach and with the assistance of alcohol, I felt I was coming to grips fairly well with my baseball loss. But my senior year brought me face to face with another loss I would be forced to endure.

One day in the summer of 1993, I came home from A&M to visit my parents for the weekend. When I walked into the house, Dad was sitting in a chair, soaking his feet in water with Epsom salt. His legs were swollen from his toes to his knees.

"What's wrong" I asked him.

"Ack, I must have worn too tight of boots when I went out hunting," he said, referring to a recent bird hunting trip.

Too tight of boots, huh? I thought, but something didn't sit right with me. He went hunting all the time and he'd never had this problem before. He was a Texan; he knew how to pick out and wear boots.

After a few days, the swelling was getting worse. He called a neighbor who was a cardiologist in Houston. Dr. Peterson came and looked him over and advised he was concerned that something was going on with my dad's heart because of the poor circulation. But the next week, after a more thorough examination in Houston, they determined it was not his heart. When a few weeks later fluid began oozing from his legs, he consulted with an internist in College Station. Since I was at A&M, I met him and my mother there. After running imaging tests, the doctor determined Dad had a tumor that was blocking a major blood artery, which was causing the blood circulation problems in his legs. He was referred to MD Anderson, the world's renowned cancer hospital in Houston.

We walked silently out to the parking lot. My dad seemed calm but confused. His blank stare gave away that he must have been scared. I was scared. The diagnosis wouldn't settle in my brain. A *cancer* hospital. My dad had cancer. He had always been invincible. He'd survived wartime in the Korean War. I hoped the internist was wrong; I hoped the tumor wasn't as bad as he'd made it sound; I hoped it was something the doctors at MD Anderson could fix quickly and easily.

I escorted them to their car, then I put my hand on his shoulder. I tried to be brave and keep my voice steady. "I love you. You gonna be okay?"

"Yes," he said, attempting the slightest smile. I think he was trying to be brave for me too.

My hoping amounted to little. The physicians at MD Anderson and a urologist in Brenham told him that the cancer had started in his colon and had spread throughout his body. There was nothing they could do.

I wondered whether I should call my brother, Ronnie, and tell him about the diagnosis, but Mom called him. By this point Ronnie was married and working in Houston as a CPA, so it was more difficult for him to take off and spend time with Dad, although he came home as often as he could. Mom and I both updated him by phone. I ached for Ronnie that he wasn't able to be with Dad as much as I knew he wanted, since he and Dad had been close.

Hospice came to my parents' house immediately and brought a bed they set up in the living room. I put everything on hold and spent as much time with him as I could. One day Dad wanted to shave. He had become very weak and frail from not having an appetite. I helped him out of bed and we walked, with me practically carrying him, to his bathroom. When we got there, he was sweaty, breathing hard, and almost ready to collapse. I hadn't given God much thought, but I knew eternity was closing in on us. I looked at Dad. His pale, thin face looked anguished and weary. "Dad, you're ready to meet Jesus, aren't you?"

He raised his face slowly. "Yes," he said with a gentle smile.

On October 22, 1993, twelve weeks after his diagnosis, the hospice nurse motioned to us that he was nearing his last breath. Mom and I gathered around the bed to say our goodbyes. I looked at my father, who had been my first coach, my constant cheerleader, and who now lay still and close to entering eternity. His body frail and his skin gray, death surrounded him. As I listened to the death rattle in his labored breathing, I thought about all the Saturday afternoons when Dad and I would watch the Game of the Week. From as far back as I could remember, it was just me and Dad, sitting in front of the TV, listening to Vin Scully announce the games, and cheering on the Dodgers or the Astros. We'd talk about the players, and I'd ask, "What do you think the pitcher's going to throw this pitch?" Dad would answer with "Oh, I bet he's going to throw a fastball." I learned so much about baseball with and because of my dad.

I gulped down a sob and whispered, "It's okay to go, Dad. I love you. Thanks for being my dad."

He was too weak to respond, but a single tear fell from his eye and rolled down his face. Then he took his last breath.

I'd lost baseball, now I had lost my dad. I felt as if someone had pushed me into a car and drove it over that cliff into the pasture all over again—only this time I couldn't relax. And this time, there were consequences. When my dad took his final breath, I felt as if I'd lost my life too.

CHAPTER 16
NOW WHAT DO I DO?

"Jon, I have a proposition for you," my mentor and old high school coach Lee Driggers said. I had called him to catch him up on my now-non-baseball career and to seek his advice on how I could break into collegiate-level coaching, since he now coached at McMurry University in Abilene, Texas. "I'd like you to come and be my assistant coach."

My jaw dropped. This was exactly what I had hoped for. If I couldn't play baseball, I wanted to coach it, which would help me stay close to the game. I'd enjoyed my time as an undergraduate assistant coach at A&M, so after graduation in 1994 with a bachelor's in kinesiology, a fancy name for physical education, I had contacted Coach Van Hook at Blinn and offered to work with his team as a pitching coach while I pursued graduate studies in kinesiology at Sam Houston State University in Huntsville, Texas, about an hour and fifteen minutes from Brenham. If I was going to coach college-level baseball, I had to have a master's degree. I worked as a pitching coach at Blinn for a year and then, in order to finish my master's more quickly, I left coaching and worked as a graduate assistant in the health and kinesiology department. Now with my master's in hand, I was itching to get back to baseball. Coach Driggers must have read my mind.

He explained that the school was building a first-class field and facility for the team, thanks to a generous donation from his uncle who had won the Florida lottery, and he needed an assistant coach. Because of our relationship and his love for me, he said I could come coach with him.

I couldn't say yes fast enough, and in the fall of 1996, I headed to Abilene. Getting to work as an adult and "equal" with my mentor was amazing. He was no longer coaching me, but I got to watch him work from the perspective of a coach rather than from a player's perspective. He and his wife, Sharon, continued to treat me kindly. They arranged for me to live for free in a garage apartment of a local physician. They even encouraged me to attend church, something I hadn't done very often since I was in high school and living with my parents.

I found a church in town that had good music and the pastor was engaging. When I attended, I couldn't explain why, but something stirred in my soul. I'd hear something and I would be so moved, I'd want to cry, or I'd feel chills run down my spine and I knew things were different here. Every Sunday that I was in town, I returned to that church. It made me feel content and helped me through each week. I felt stronger and more at peace, but I couldn't explain what it was or why. I'd certainly never experienced anything like it at my home church when I was growing up, although every once in a while, I'd feel those chills there too. I wanted more. It felt good. I'd always feel as though I was riding on a high coming out of church. Almost like getting drunk—but without the alcohol, vomiting, and subsequent hangovers.

For a year I worked with Coach Driggers and I enjoyed it—but in the back of my mind I knew I didn't want to be an assistant coach for the rest of my life. My dream was to be a head coach at a big-time university. I wanted to run the team, I wanted to make the decisions, I wanted to win back my status of being somebody. But the deeper into the coaching part of baseball I went, the more I saw the dark side of it. Going to coaching association events and interacting with other coaches from all around the country, I started to feel that familiar sense of not belonging. Many of the coaches seemed to thrive on using obnoxious profanity and arguing with umpires. They seemed to be arrogant, sexist, political people who thought they knew everything. I hated to see what they were doing to the game I loved.

This isn't the kind of people I want to associate with for the rest of my career, I realized. *I want to experience baseball, but not this way.* Coach Driggers was upstanding and an exception, but I even saw some of the politics he had to deal with, and that turned me off too. I liked the coaching part, I liked helping the players get better and cheering on the team, but not all the other stuff that went with it.

On top of that, a few people who were close to me commented that I would never make any money coaching—even at the collegiate level. Their opinion really mattered to me, and it got me thinking about my future. I started to doubt myself all over again. Was I choosing the right career? What if I became a coach and I wasn't that good?

Okay, what am I going to do now? I wondered. I was losing yet another dream as I watched baseball slip through my fingers again.

While I was working toward my master's degree at Sam Houston, I'd really gotten into school. *I can be a professor at a university*, I thought. *That could be cool.* I decided to go back to school and get my doctorate. Being a professor was respectable and seemed like a good life. Although professors weren't rich, they had a nice lifestyle, and I figured I could be content in academia. So after a year working with Coach Driggers, in the fall of 1997, I started my doctorate studies in kinesiology at Louisiana State University.

I enjoyed LSU and working on my Ph.D. But soon I again began to doubt my career choice. I was studying the same material as my master's, just a little more in detail. And I couldn't shake the reality that I would be in school for three to four more years and I was going to be so far in debt from school loans that I would be paying on them until I was retired and dead. So coaching wouldn't offer me a comfortable lifestyle, and academia would keep me poor too because of the loans.

I felt frustrated and afraid. Baseball had let me down, and I felt as if I was wandering around, flapping loosely like a flag in the wind, never calm, never content, never secure.

Now what? I wondered. I wasn't going to church anymore, but didn't think that offered any real solutions either. I thought maybe I needed to focus on a career that *would* make a lot of money. Rich people seemed happy.

While I was considering exactly what that money-making career might be, I had a conversation with a friend of my brother who was in pharmaceutical sales. I knew they made money, and he seemed happy.

He got me an interview with his company, and I knocked the interview out of the park. *I got this*, I told myself, finally feeling confident after I hadn't for so long. When they offered me a position, I took it. The company gave me a large territory, and I was on the road 85 percent of the time, living mostly in hotels. But I liked it—I liked the competition and I was good at it. I especially liked it when my boss would call me month after month and say, "Jon, you broke another record this month."

For as well as I was doing and as much as I liked the travel and the perks and the money, I had no friends, because even when I was in town, if I met somebody I'd be gone again. I had great money, but nothing to spend it on, and I wanted to settle down. I was ready to meet a girl and fall in love. I wanted normal things; I was ready for a "normal" life. So I left that company in 1998, not sure what I really wanted to do. I found a job in Houston in the insurance industry, hopeful that I could make great money, settle down, and finally find the happiness that had eluded me. Everything seemed to click at first. I worked as an auto adjuster, then they moved me onto the national catastrophe team for homeowners. Unfortunately, that meant I had to go where natural catastrophes had been—hurricanes, earthquakes, tornados, hailstorms—and that meant more travel. I liked it because I got to travel with a team and I liked the team, but I still felt unsettled and still searching who I was and what I wanted to do with my life.

I was at a turning point. Letting go of baseball, which I had been involved with for almost twenty years, left me stranded in a world that was moving at sonic speed. It seemed like the faster I went, the further away others moved. The more I searched, the more others found. The more I wanted, the more they obtained. As I attempted to become part of society, the further I fell behind in what the world was doing. And the harder I tried to catch up, the more exhausted my whole being was becoming. I was left in the dust, breathing the exhaust fumes others were leaving behind.

I didn't know who I was anymore and what other talents I had—or even if I had other talents. The worst part was hearing about old teammates who had gone on in the game and how the god of baseball had blessed them. James Nix, an amazing pitcher and my sidekick in high school, was drafted by the Cincinnati Reds. John Schulte, from our high school team, got drafted by the Pittsburgh Pirates as an outfielder/middle infielder. He could run like a deer and had a cannon as an arm. Keith Schmidt, a boy from Burton, one of Brenham's neighboring towns, would often play ball with us while I was growing up. He was drafted by the Baltimore Orioles as an outfielder. Craig Bolcerek, the catcher my senior year in high school, was drafted by the Texas Rangers, but chose to stay in Brenham and work with his father at their fencing company. None of them were playing in the majors, but most were playing in the minor leagues and that was something special. I didn't begrudge any of them for their good fortune. They were strong and great players. But I couldn't help but wonder, *Why not me? What happened that they get to play and I'm out of baseball and stuck trying to figure out what I should do with my life?*

Drinking numbed the pain and gave me a sense of worthiness for a while. When I was drunk, I was somebody once again. People liked me and I was confident. But the effects of alcohol always wore off, leaving me alone again, with my condemning thoughts and regrets.

I was not interested in temporary relief. I had found ways for that already and, though that had worked for short periods, I found myself empty-hearted with the same feelings when it was all said and done. I was in search of a permanent solution—something I could rely on to make my internal combustion go away and never come back. I was willing to try anything—it was not as if things could get any worse.

I had lots of money, but it too failed to bring me lasting happiness. I could buy what I wanted when I wanted. But after a while, I was working long and hard hours and buying things soon lost their appeal for me.

Perhaps a person would bring me happiness and offer me the fulfillment that I desperately wanted and sought. But I didn't even have a girlfriend. And really, what could I offer somebody else? Why would anybody want me? I was an unhappy, messed-up loser—that's how I saw myself.

In October 2002, my brother called. "Jon, I've got the girl for you. Her name is Stephanie. I work with her dad, and we think the two of you would hit it off. We think y'all would be a good fit. Her dad showed me a picture of her. She's blonde, athletic, and seems really sweet. If you are interested, here's her phone number."

I wasn't sure about getting set up, but I also knew I needed something in my life. Perhaps she was it?

Finally after a few nights, I wrestled up my courage and called her. We talked for thirty to forty-five minutes, just getting acquainted. The conversation flowed well and she was easy to talk with. She was a middle school physical education teacher and also coached volleyball and track. I was definitely intrigued and wanted to meet her. But rather than do the same-old *let's go out for dinner and drink* routine, I decided to try something unique.

"How about I come to one of your volleyball games? During the game I'll sit among the fans and you can guess who I am. Then after the game I'll walk up to you and introduce myself." I wanted it to be mysterious and fun to have her wonder, *I'm going to meet someone new tonight but I have no clue what he looks like. I wonder who he could be?* Not only would it be fun, but also more relaxed. "After the game," I continued, "we can get something to eat and get to know each other better."

"That sounds great!"

A few days later, I showed up at her school's gymnasium. The game was scheduled for 5:00 p.m. and I arrived early. I walked in to the gym, feeling anxious. My palms were sweaty and my face felt flushed.

Get it together, man! I told myself. *It's just a girl, no big deal.* But it was a big deal. I wanted to appear calm and cool, like I was just there to watch my kid play. I walked up the bleachers and settled in about halfway up and waited.

As parents started to arrive and take their places, I was still so nervous I failed to notice that I had chosen the visitors' side of the court. The visiting team playing against Stephanie's school was predominantly black. Stephanie's school was predominantly white. And I stuck out like the proverbial sore thumb. So much for being inconspicuous.

As soon as Stephanie walked into the gym with her team, my eyes found her. She was wearing black pants, ankle-length black boots, and a tucked-in white shirt with their school logo on the left, below her shoulder. She was thin, and her straight blonde hair laid just past her shoulders. Her body was fit and athletic—I knew she'd played soccer in college. And my brother was right, she did look sweet and innocent. I was immediately attracted to her.

I watched the game—but mostly her—and was impressed by her coaching style. She encouraged her girls by clapping and talking with them in a supportive way.

She might be the one, I found myself thinking.

After the match, which her team won, I walked down to the court and waited while she and the girls took down the volleyball net and put the volleyballs and chairs away. Then she walked to me, wearing a big smile.

As we introduced ourselves, she laughed and said, "I knew exactly who you were when you sat down. You sat right in the middle of the other team's parents so it wasn't hard to pick you out."

I laughed too. "Yeah, I guess I should have found a better place to sit."

We went to dinner at Texas Land & Cattle and talked for an hour and a half while we ate. We talked like we had known each other for years, and she made me feel so at ease and comfortable with her. Her voice was calm and she listened attentively and acted like she cared about what I was saying.

After we ate, I walked her to her vehicle, gave her a hug, told her how much I enjoyed meeting her, and that I'd like to see her again. She immediately agreed.

She is so sweet, I thought on the drive home. *I can definitely see myself with her.*

The next day I called my brother and told him that I enjoyed meeting her and I was probably in gaga and goo-goo land! He laughed and told me that she came from a good family and she was the real deal. The more time I spent with Stephanie, the more hooked I became. I went from thinking, *This might be the one,* to thinking, *She is definitely the one.*

I was continually amazed that she was into me—*me*. She didn't think I was a loser. Her faith in me had nothing to do with my high school baseball celebrity status.

Everything was going well, we were both in love, and in September 2003, eleven months later, we were married. I had finally found my happiness.

CHAPTER 17
TROUBLE IN PARADISE

"I can get rid of you as fast as I married you." The words popped out of my mouth before I realized what I was saying.

Stephanie reacted with surprise and hurt, but said nothing as I grabbed the camera from her and started taking photos of the luau we were attending. I didn't feel she was taking photos fast enough to suit me, and so I wanted her to *know* how much she had disappointed me. But really it wasn't about capturing those photographic moments that got me so riled.

We were newly married and she was pregnant. I wanted to have kids, I wanted to be a father, but I was afraid of all the responsibility that came with a family. What if I was a terrible dad? I'd screwed up my life; what would keep me from doing the same to our baby? That terrified me.

Our daughter, Kylie, was born April 19, 2004, and she was the most beautiful baby, but I was so busy being self-centered, I couldn't appreciate her sweet little life. Stephanie took to being a great mom. I wanted to parent alongside Stephanie, but I saw how much better she was at it and my insecurities kicked in again.

The more she tried to include me in the joy of our new family, the more resentful I became. My moods would swing unpredictably and my emotions became toxic. I would yell at her for any little thing—like not taking photos fast enough—but underneath the anger was that deep-seated fear, which had been my faithful companion from as far back as I could remember.

Stephanie was patient and kind with me, and I knew she loved me, but I just couldn't accept that she did—or could. The combination of my fear of her rejection and my flawed, worthless thinking of being less than and never good enough were a lethal mixture as the rants and raves of sarcasm echoed off the walls of her heart. As I reacted harshly to her, she responded with a quietness and an ache of not understanding what was happening or how to fix it. That made me even angrier, because I saw her as being too good and too strong for me. It was not a display of confidence but rather a lashing out toward her in hopes of making the playing surface level. To bring her down to my level—I believed that was the only chance of us having the deep intimacy I was searching for. I wanted her to fill the hole that had been in my soul, the hole that baseball and academia and money had failed to fill.

If she couldn't fill it, what could? I'd run out of options. Though we were attending church, I never considered that God might be able to fill that hole. Religion felt empty and dry. God seemed far away, and anyway, I believed he was too busy judging me to consider actually helping me out.

I turned once again to my good friend who had come to my rescue in so many situations in the past: alcohol. When I met Stephanie, I didn't feel the need to continue drinking as I had, but I became so consumed with what a failure I was, it didn't take much to twist my arm and persuade me back to that kind of lifestyle. Alcohol made me forget all the shame and guilt I felt. When I drank, everybody liked me. They respected me. I was *somebody* again.

But it didn't last, so I would have to keep drinking. After work, I started stopping at a convenience store and picking up two sixteen-ounce cans of Busch beer so I could handle the evenings at home.

Then one afternoon while I was out mowing my lawn, I stopped to chat with my neighbor, who was holding a thirty-two-ounce Styrofoam cup.

"Hey, what are you drinking there?" I said, just to make conversation.

"Diet Coke," he said and smiled. Then he added, "With Captain Morgan."

"What's that?"

"Spiced rum. You ought to try it."

"Yeah, okay. Make me one."

He walked into his house and within minutes, he was back out, carrying a Styrofoam cup filled with ice and the drink.

It was smooth and sweet. I liked it. The next day I stopped at the liquor store, picked up some spiced rum and started drinking Captain Morgan.

Every day after work, instead of dealing with Stephanie and Kylie, I would pour myself a smooth rum and Diet Coke. I began to look forward to the end of the workday when I could ply myself with my elixir of life, because once I poured that drink, I was cool and relaxed, and all was well. Everything was wonderful. Even better was that I didn't suffer the nausea, vomiting, or headaches I'd experienced with the other drinks. It didn't matter how much spiced rum I put in, my body could handle it.

I had switched jobs and was now working at an insurance agency. It was going great. I was making a lot of money, and my family life was good—because I was drinking all my troubles away. What could be better?

But my family life wasn't good. I was still the same old Jon— the guy who struggled to contain my anger and insecurities; the guy who would pop off with some sarcastic, demeaning comment whenever I was unhappy. As I continued with my unappreciative, explosive behavior, Stephanie began spending more and more time with her family. They were loving and supportive and took great care of Kylie. But I didn't see it that way. I felt threatened that she preferred them to me. So one afternoon, after a particularly heated discussion with her about her family, I decided, *Why should I wait until I get home to drink? It would be better to be calm and relaxed before I arrive. That way I'm good to go as soon as I walk through the door.*

So I stopped at the liquor store and picked up a bottle of Captain Morgan—a special bottle that would stay in my truck. Then I hopped over to the convenience store, bought a Big Gulp-size of Diet Coke, filled it halfway, and then once I was back in my vehicle, I topped it off with rum. That forty-five minute commute was the best I'd ever had.

After that as soon as I got in my truck at the end of every workday, I stopped at the closest convenience store and got my Diet Coke. Or I'd stop at Sonic, order a large Diet Coke, pour out half, and then fill it up with my liquid friend.

Every night I felt in control, confident, and calm, but the morning always came, and with it the same dreaded feelings: *Man, you are worthless, you're fat, you aren't any good. You're a terrible father. You're an awful husband. You're a complete and total disgrace.*

I desperately needed to drown out those condemning thoughts that now seemed to plague me all day long. One morning at work at about 10:30, when those thoughts returned, I found myself daydreaming about that Captain Morgan bottle that was just outside in the parking lot. I'd never had a drink while working, but what harm would it do? Just a nip to tide me over. It would be easy to hide since everyone would just think I was sipping a soda.

The rush it gave me! I was able to get away with drinking and *nobody knew.* I liked the way it made me feel, I mean I had confidence and people *liked* me. In fact, one guy liked me well enough to invite me to go drinking with him after work. His wife traveled a lot for her job, so my colleague and I regularly headed over to Hooter's or to his house after work for drinks. Stephanie never knew—she was at her mom and dad's house anyway, so I justified my absence from home saying that she was out of it just as much as I was.

To my surprise, I came home from work one day to find Stephanie sitting on the couch.

"I need to talk to you," she said, sounding nervous.

"What's up?" I said and sat on a chair across from her.

She was quiet for a moment, looking down at her hands. Then she inhaled deeply and blurted out, "I'm pregnant."

My jaw dropped open as I tried to grasp what she was saying. *How is that possible?* I thought. She's on the pill. I knew the pill wasn't 100 percent effective, and I knew I bore as much responsibility as she did. But it was easier on my ego to get upset with her.

"I forgot to take the pill. That's when it must have happened." She wouldn't look at me, as though she were afraid I would get angry and throw something or storm out of the house.

Is that what she thinks of me? Yes, it was. And I had only myself to blame.

I sighed. *Great. Just what we need to get our marriage back on track.* It wasn't that I didn't want this child. I had fallen in love with Kylie and knew this baby would be wonderful too. But I knew deep down we needed to work on our marriage, and I needed to work on my issues before we had another kid. Plus my mind went to the financial aspect. *How much is this going to cost? Kids are expensive.* I was making a good living, but I wanted to spend the money on stuff *I* wanted, not on diapers.

Looking at Stephanie's fearful expression, I knew I needed to change my attitude. I was determined to make this pregnancy better for her than how I'd handled her pregnancy with Kylie. "Okay," I told her. "We'll make this work. Somehow."

In her first trimester, she miscarried. As she grieved the sudden loss of our child, I also grieved. But I wouldn't let her see me cry, so she never knew how hard I took her miscarriage. I just couldn't bring myself to share our pain together. I felt as if I needed to be strong in front of her, otherwise, she'd think I was weak.

One afternoon, when she was crying and I failed to comfort her, I saw how pained she was—not just over the baby, but over my failures as a husband. I took a long walk and had a heart-to-heart with myself. *I'd better start working on this marriage real quick or she's going to leave me and it's not going to be good.*

We became more serious about attending church together. I didn't get much out of it, but it felt like the thing to do. I also suggested we go to marriage counseling—I believed that would show her and everybody that I was serious about my commitment to her and that I was the bigger, better person. But so many times at counseling I wasn't real. I would blame Stephanie for all our problems and justify why I was behaving a certain way. I could never let my pride go and be vulnerable because I thought my heart was about to get cut wide open. Especially when Stephanie told the counselor that she thought I drank too much.

"No, that's crazy," I said, defending myself. "I don't drink that often, and when I do, I can control it. I can quit anytime I want."

In fact, I had quit. Several times. I'd wake up, look at myself in the mirror, and announce, "Today I'm not drinking." And I'd quit . . . until that afternoon when I'd start to crave the taste and the sensation of the alcohol in my system. Oh how it untangled my nerves. "Man, I've got to have something." And the craving would nag at me until I gave in.

Each night I'd feel such hatred toward myself, I'd pray, "God, don't let me wake up tomorrow. I don't want to wake up. I'm worthless."

Then I'd wake up, and I'd start the game all over. "Okay, I'm not drinking." I'd even get into a little negotiation match with God. "You know I really need to sell something at work. So if I quit drinking, let me sell something." And then by three o'clock, I was drinking again.

But still I refused to come clean about it with Stephanie— or with anybody. I felt like if I told her the truth and that I was sorry, I would show her how weak I was, and that she would take that knowledge and use it against me to run right over me. She'd think, *He appears to be a tough guy, but he's really weak. He's so weak, he's ridiculous.*

I couldn't—I *wouldn't*—have her think that about me. Did she understand that plenty of people respected me and thought I was a strong, "got it all together" kind of guy? People at my job constantly sought me out for advice and encouragement. They wanted my help, and I loved helping them. But Stephanie didn't seem to need my help. Why would she? I worked it up in my mind to believe that she had her family to help her out. She had her friends. She had our child. She didn't want me. And those thoughts crushed me.

Even though our relationship was strained, I still loved her and wanted her to love me. The pill had started to make Stephanie feel sick, so she stopped taking it. We tried to be careful, but soon she became pregnant again. I think we both hoped this child would help us get our lives together.

But so far, nothing was changing. By December 2006, when Kylie wasn't quite yet three years old, Stephanie and I were barely speaking to each other. It was miserable, but at least my job was going well. I looked forward to my company's annual Christmas party for employees only, where I could be around people who liked me and wanted me to share their holiday joy, something I felt I was lacking at home.

The party was on a Friday at an Italian restaurant. Our employer gave us the afternoon off so everyone could meet at the restaurant around noon. That morning I left the house for work at my regular time, completed a few tasks at the office, and left early to head over to my drinking buddy's house. Conveniently enough, his wife was out of town again. By ten o'clock, he and I had already thrown back several rounds of Crown Royal mixed with a few splashes of Coke. Then we headed out and stopped at a convenience store for a few beers.

"Want to grab something to eat too?" my friend asked.

"Nah, I'm good," I told him. When I drank I didn't eat because I felt full and bloated, but also because I preferred to fill my gut with alcohol to feel high rather than take up that stomach space with food.

By the time we arrived at the party, I was feeling on top of the world. Everybody there received a two-drink ticket limit because the company wanted to make sure nobody got out of control. That was like an invitation to me! I sweet-talked the liquor ladies into letting me have as many drink tickets as I wanted. And I got loaded.

As the employees ate, I drank. As they mingled and chatted, I drank. By the time they held their Christmas sing-along, I was more than ready to join in.

The song leader divided the group into twelve sections so we could all sing "The Twelve Days of Christmas." I was in group seven with the "seven swans a swimming." I was so plastered I don't remember what I did, but afterward people kept coming up to me, laughing, and saying, "Jon, you were really going crazy during that song!"

I thanked them and laughed it off, but a terrible thought began to nag at me: I couldn't *remember* what I'd done that was so crazy.

Several hours into the party, sharp pains from my right side started shooting through my torso. I said my goodbyes and headed out to the parking lot, figuring I'd go home and sleep it off. When I hit the bright sunlight of the afternoon, however, everything around me began to spin and the all-too-familiar nausea showed up. I doubled over as every ounce of liquid gushed out of my mouth. I couldn't stop vomiting. Down to my knees I fell and then I became too weak even to keep my head up as I retched and retched in a grassy area of one of the parking lot's medians.

Some ladies from the office were leaving the party and saw me. One of the women was able to retrieve my cell phone and called Stephanie, who was still at school working. She told them she'd be there as quickly as she could. But at that time of the day, and with her being at least thirty miles away, it took her an hour to get there. The women stayed with me to make sure I was okay, but all I could do was groan and dry heave.

When she finally arrived, all three of them tried to get me into Stephanie's Nissan Maxima to take me home. But I couldn't sit up without starting to vomit again. By this point Mike Hotchkiss and Ken Hotchkiss, brothers whose father owned the agency, were leaving the party and saw the commotion. Mike got his suburban and lowered all the seats so I could lie down. Then he and Ken grabbed my arms and legs and placed me into the back of his suburban.

"We're taking you to the hospital," Ken said.

"No! I don't need to go to the hospital," I said, feeling angry and confused. *Great,* I thought. *Of everybody who could see me like this, it had to be the owner's sons.*

"Look," Mike said. "Something isn't right. You just passed out and you're are vomiting!"

"I'll be okay," I said, still feeling weak and nauseated.

They wouldn't listen to me, though, and took me to the emergency room at Cypress Fairbanks Medical Center in Houston, with Stephanie following behind. But I don't remember that trip either.

The next morning I woke up and couldn't swallow without pain. A large tube was stuck down my throat. I felt like a truck had run over me and then backed up and did it again. My entire body ached.

Where am I? I glanced around the stark, white room, but couldn't see anything to give me some sense of where I was and why. I could see through some glass into a hallway. And on a wall across the hall I spotted a sign. I couldn't make out much of it, but I definitely saw "ICU" in big letters. I was in the intensive care unit.

What is this? What's going on?

Eventually a nurse came in to check on me, but she wasn't helpful in giving me any information. Nobody was there with me. I was alone. I felt awful. And I *couldn't remember* what had happened.

Sometime later that morning Mike and Ken came to see me.

"Hey, Jon," Mike said. "How are you doing?"

"What's going on?" I asked, feeling very sober.

"You must have had too much to drink yesterday," Ken said.

The previous day flashed through my mind. Pieces of scenes were fuzzy, but I did recall that I'd had a lot to drink. All day long.

Oh, that's not good, I realized. *I can't control this.* But I couldn't understand why I was in the ICU and my wife wasn't with me. "Where's Stephanie?"

"Stephanie was here last night," Mike said. "She's probably around here taking a walk."

"You were acting like you were in serious pain in your side," Ken explained. "We didn't know if your appendix burst or what was going on." They explained what had happened and how they were involved—none of which I remembered.

Mike nodded. "When Stephanie was talking with the doctors, they told her, 'We've lost many people just like this, and we don't know if we can get him back. We don't know what's all in his system.'"

"Jon, your wife lost it then," Ken said.

I had overdosed on alcohol. Hearing those words, *We don't know if we can get him back,* and thinking about what that must of done to Stephanie made me feel even sicker than I already did. I didn't want to hurt her. We were struggling in our marriage, but deep down, I still loved her—and I still wanted her to love and respect me. *Well, man, this certainly isn't the way to do that.*

Not long after Mike and Ken left, Stephanie came in. She looked exhausted. Her puffy eyes had dark circles around them as if she hadn't slept. *You did this to her,* my mind accused.

"How are you feeling?" she asked. She seemed tentative.

I shrugged. "Okay, I guess." I was so embarrassed by what I had done. I was ruining everything for everybody.

Stephanie sat beside me the entire time. She didn't judge or ridicule me. She didn't ask for an explanation or an apology. She was a loving and supportive wife. I wanted to apologize, but I couldn't. I just couldn't come clean about what I'd done. It gnawed at me and sent my thoughts into overdrive, *What a loser. You can't even keep your alcohol down. You failed at the Tylenol overdose, you failed as a baseball player, you're failing as a husband. You fail at everything!*

We sat in silence, accompanied only by the sound of the monitors taking my blood pressure and keeping track of my heart rate and blood oxygen levels.

Saturday evening the staff moved me out of ICU to a regular floor to continue monitoring me. Because I had so much alcohol in my system, the detox process could kill me as much as the overdosing could.

By Sunday I was going out of my mind. My body felt awful and I couldn't stand not being able to get up and do anything. "Man, I got to get out of here," I kept saying, but nobody seemed to pay much attention to that demand.

I didn't get released until Sunday evening, with Stephanie there the entire time. But even when we went home, I never said anything about Friday's episode, and Stephanie didn't ask.

The only thing she did ask was, "How do you feel?"

I kept telling her I was sore.

"I'm so sorry you're sore." She seemed genuine, as if she really meant it. That made me feel even worse. That Sunday night I was sitting at my desk and I wanted so badly to tell her how sorry I was for what I'd done. Just to say simply, "I'm sorry." And I was so upset at myself because I could not do it.

I'll write her a letter, I decided. *If she could just read this letter, she'd forgive me and things would be okay.* So I pulled out a pad of paper and began to spill my thoughts. I wrote that I was sorry, that I appreciated her support, that I knew I put her through hell and back, and on and on. After I was done, I folded it and put it in the back of my desk. I'd give it to her the next day, I promised myself. But the next day came and once again I couldn't face the truth of what I'd done and who I had become. So in the drawer the letter remained and I pretended that it hadn't affected me.

Deep down it *had* affected me. It killed me not telling her the truth, but I was too embarrassed and full of pride. It would prove everything I'd known—that she was better than me, that I was a failure and a terrible husband. I'd be admitting it! There she was, standing right by me, and I was afraid of saying just two simple, little words: *I'm sorry*.

We never said another word about it. But our relationship seemed to soften. We still weren't in a good place, but my near-death experience caused us both to be kinder toward each other.

And if I had any concerns about was happening at work, I encountered the same response. Sure, people said they were glad I was back, but no one confronted me about what had happened. A few even eventually joked with me about it—"Boy, you got loaded that night!" "Geesh, we give you two drinks and look at you!" Then they'd tell me something funny or outrageous I'd done—none of which I could remember—and we'd all laugh. I started to think, *I was the life of the party. That was pretty cool. Yeah, that's me.* Somehow the shame of my actions faded away and in my mind I rewrote the events to make me appear not so appalling.

So I didn't feel too terrible the next time I stopped at that convenience store, picked up another Diet Coke, added some rum, and enjoyed my night cap on the way home from work.

CHAPTER 18
ANOTHER LETDOWN

When our son, Jake, was born on January 12, 2007, I was determined to be the kind of father I needed to be.

But the road to hell is paved with good intentions, so the saying goes. Stephanie and I planned together to buy a new house and for her to quit her job as a middle school teacher so she could stay home with the kids, a move that kept me up at night wondering how we were going to manage financially. We would be okay on one salary, but that wasn't the point to my mind. I felt the pressure of not having enough money for *me*.

And as much as I intended to be this "new" man, I didn't work on our marriage, and I didn't become a good husband, and I didn't tame my drinking. Instead again, I picked at every little thing. I'd walk into the house and see all the toys strewn all over and immediately I'd pop off at her, "What do you do all day? You don't work, can't you at least keep the house in order?" Or dinner would not be prepared and I'd say, "This is great. I work all day to bring home the bacon and I have to cook for myself. Really?"

I didn't want to see how busy Stephanie was staying or what a good job she was actually doing. Nothing was ever good enough for me.

Yet again too soon my soul ached from its void and unhappiness, and too soon I returned to my old habits and blamed Stephanie for all my problems.

One day, I came home from work to find her on the computer. "What are you doing?"

"I'm on Facebook," she said.

What's she doing on Facebook? I didn't like it. I'd heard about the trouble people could get into on social media when they reconnected with old flames and then had affairs.

"What are you up to?"

"I like catching up with people. I just want to see what they're doing in their lives."

I wasn't convinced. Day and night I kept dwelling on her being on Facebook, certain she was reaching out to someone for love and compassion. Soon I convinced myself, *She is cheating on me.* I began imagining that while I was at work, some guy was at our house, that they were alone together and they were sharing secrets, that she was telling him how awful and weak and disgusting I was. My mind went into overdrive until I completely believed everything I imagined. I was convinced she was having an affair and she was going to leave me.

She's not going to get away with that, I told myself. *She can't leave me if I leave her first.* In February 2009, without ever saying a word to Stephanie, without confronting her or finding out what the truth really was, I contacted a divorce attorney. Once again, I was cocked and ready to explode. I was reverting back to my MO to run away instead of buckle down, recommit, and see the tough times through.

The night before she was to receive the divorce papers, I got home and found her in the kitchen area doing laundry.

"Hey, you're going to get some papers served to you soon."

She didn't say anything, and I walked to my office. We didn't speak the rest of the night.

The next day, while I was at work, a deputy sheriff arrived at our house and handed her the divorce papers.

She responded to me this time. She emailed me. "I can't believe you're walking out on us. I've been loyal and supportive to you, and you're doing this to us."

Blah, blah, blah, I thought, building my case against her. *No, you're not. Don't lie to me.* But the truth was, I didn't want to get divorced. I wanted our marriage to work; I just didn't know how to do that and I was too hurt by what I believed she had done to me.

I moved out of the house and in with the mother of a drinking buddy of mine, who was also in the process of getting a divorce. We were free to drown our sorrows and build our cases against the women who had disrespected us.

Around that time I had a client who offered me a glass of Diet Coke and vodka. I'd never had vodka before. As soon as I drank it, I thought, *This is the bomb here! This is so much better than Captain Morgan.*

"What kind is this?" I asked him.

"Popov." He chuckled. "We drink so much vodka around here that we need to buy the cheap stuff. It's good, as you can tell, and you can get it in a big plastic bottle."

The next day I went to a liquor store and replaced Captain Morgan with Popov. It cost ten dollars for two liters. And since it was in a plastic bottle, I just kept it under my seat, where I knew I could drink it any time I wanted.

In addition to drinking the vodka, I drank a lot of red wine. I'd go to Walmart, get the cheapest bottle of wine, drink the whole bottle, and then follow it up with the vodka.

Baseball had been my god, but it let me down. Now alcohol was god; money was god; control was god. As long as my life was working, I was okay. But my life wasn't working. Everything was falling apart.

My marriage was over, my kids barely knew me, my job was suffering, I had lost friends, and I could no longer control any of it.

Each night after work I drank all evening, and the morning followed with sluggish and lifeless feelings contrasting with someone who used to be an early riser and full of energy years before. Motivating myself to crawl out of bed and go to work was becoming a daunting chore. I had little to no desire to leave the house and be part of society, since that meant I had to put on my game face and pretend to be interested in others. Although I cared about what others were feeling and sharing with me, my self-centeredness had completely taken over and I found myself becoming irritated with their continuous belly-aching. I would think, *It's not all about you. I have problems too.*

Our divorce was finalized on March 14, 2010. In the spring. This season had always been my favorite because the winter temperatures had departed and, of course, baseball season was in full swing. On any given night, I would stop by a ballpark and watch kids play the game I had grown up loving. But now, instead of watching baseball, I was content to go home and drink. I had lost interest in the game. Instead of leaving work and going home to my wife and kids, I went home each night to an empty, quiet house. My name was no longer written toward the top of the leaderboard at work either.

As I continued to muddle my way through my mess, a deep and pervasive loneliness absorbed me. My life was definitely not what I had expected it to be. Nothing was going my way. When I'd drink, the tension of my tangled nerves and thoughts began to ease. Like the sun hitting the morning dew, all my pent-up stress and worries seemed to dissipate in an instant. There was a ray of hope shining brightly through the pellets of ice, Diet Coke, and vodka. And as my mouth touched the smooth, sweet sensation of the contents in the cup, a warm and relaxing assurance comforted my whole body and, for once, it felt like paradise.

The fears of how others viewed me were nonexistent as fearless courage circulated through my bloodstream. Loneliness vanished into thin air. It was magical. Just as I used to feel about baseball, alcohol didn't let me down. Regardless of what

I said or did, it never sailed away like past friendships. Nor did it judge or scorn me. It did not care if I made it big-time in baseball or in any other occupation. And it did not care if I had one hundred friends or just one. It listened without speaking any words, and it never changed its effect on me. It loved me just the way I was—that was a first.

But then things began to change. The more time we spent together and the more I obsessed about and consumed my drink, the less growth our friendship encountered. My pessimistic outlook and feelings of doubt, guilt, and shame were returning—even while I was drinking. Instead of filling my needs, I felt more and more isolated and discouraged, as though even the alcohol was laughing at me.

Every day, every week, was the same thing; drinking had become a seemingly impossible habit to break. My reflection showed a swollen, red-faced basket case repeating the same words each and every morning: "I am not drinking today. That's it. I am done." Regardless of the promises and plea bargains I made, however, the cravings would come back and, once again, I was no longer in control. *More*, my insane mind yelled at me. *Give me more!*

I reacted by giving it what it wanted—and hating myself because of it. I drank even more vodka, but it no longer took away my pain. It no longer let me forget the anger, jealousy, fear, shame, insecurity, and guilt I struggled with. Alcohol too had let me down.

A family filled with so much promise, love, and hope was splintered apart by a husband and a father afraid of responsibilities. A job that was secure and fruitful was on the brink of collapse because of a lack of gratitude and a desire to be challenged. Friendships that were genuine and real were walking away from the drastic ups and downs in my behavior, never knowing which Jon was showing up. And a life was nearly bankrupt from self-centered thoughts and actions. It was not about the alcohol at all—it was all about me.

It was time for it to be over. The pain was not worth it anymore. I had searched for ways to be happy and nothing had worked. It seemed like everything I touched turn to dust and ruin. Relationships, baseball, prestige, exercise, money, and alcohol—they had all failed to give me anything to hold on to. They came and they went, here for a while and then gone.

I was done with it all. I'd almost accidentally killed myself once before with an alcohol overdose, perhaps I could succeed at it this time.

Early in the morning on March 26, 2010, I headed to the liquor store and stocked up on vodka and Diet Coke. Then I went back to my lonely house, where I now lived, after Stephanie and the kids moved away. I closed all the blinds in the house and went into the kitchen. It was midmorning when I grabbed a large Styrofoam cup, dropped ice and Diet Coke into it, then filled it with vodka. I placed it on an end table next to my brown leather recliner in the family room, then I grabbed the whole bottle of vodka and placed that on the floor by me, so I could grab it without looking and refill my cup.

I dropped into my recliner, propped up my feet, grabbed the remote control, and turned on ESPN. I drank and watched sports. I drank and surfed the internet. I drank and channel surfed. The only times I got up were for bathroom breaks or to grab more to drink, and then I was back at it.

For sixteen hours straight, I drank.

CHAPTER 19
ROCK BOTTOM

The clock on the TV's DVR said 2:30 a.m.

I had dozed off and on briefly in the recliner, but for a solid sixteen hours I downed every ounce of alcohol in my house. And I was *still* alive.

Now I was restless and irritable. The calm and good feeling had worn off. Grabbing a firm hold on the cushioned arms, I raised myself up and yelled furiously toward the ceiling, "Why is this happening to me? Why? What am I doing wrong?" I was at my wits' end and the pain was unbearable. Tears flowed as I gasped for air in the middle of each sob. "Please, God! I want this to be over. What good am I here? Please?"

Silence answered me.

For so long I had grasped at straws of happiness with hopes of grabbing something that would make me feel better, yet I kept coming up empty-handed. All I had obtained had been temporary. I had done everything I could think of to get me out of this pitiful, awful state of mind. This was not where I wanted to be. I had ruined everything in my life. I felt even worse than when I'd tried to commit suicide by swallowing all those Tylenols when I was in high school. I was miserable then, but I had only really messed up my own life. Now I had a family I couldn't even hold together. I was screwing up a lot of other people's lives. I couldn't bear the thought.

They would be so much better off without me, I thought, wishing I had another glass of vodka in the house that I could drown myself in.

For some reason, however, my heart was still beating and I was still breathing. "Why?" I repeated the single word over and over. Why was I still alive? Why had I made such a mess of my life? Why did I have no control over my life? Why could I not fill that aching emptiness and feel at peace with myself? Why had God not answered me?

I had hit rock bottom.

I'd heard enough about how drinking could destroy a person's life, along with those the person had injured. Lives marked with so much promise had been ruined, leaving victims behind to deal with reconciling and cleaning up the aftermath. Even though when I drank I knew one wrong turn had the potential of wreaking havoc and inflicting pain on so many, but the mind-altering effects of alcohol had always resulted in a feeling of invincibility—if nothing bad had happened yet, what was going to happen now? It was never going to happen to me.

But it did happen to me. I couldn't hide my faults any longer. And I didn't want to. I didn't want to pretend that everything was all right when I was dying inside. I didn't want to ache any more. For once in my life, the consequences were here.

I had lived a life of self-centeredness for long enough. And I had no one to blame but myself. Whether my situation came about because of the way I was raised, the people I associated with, or the events that had taken place, it didn't matter anymore. Blaming others had not helped solve any of my issues. If anything, it caused more problems. If I wanted things to change, I was the one who had to change.

I had actually performed my best during some of the most pressure-filled moments. I'd thrived in situations when the heartbeat of the baseball stadium had paused and it depended on me to jumpstart it. I had always come through, passing with flying colors. But as much as I tried now to come through, I couldn't; I was falling apart.

I knew I needed to change and I knew I had to be the one to do it, but how? I'd tried to change in the past and look where it had gotten me: sitting in a dark living room, alone, drinking myself to a death that refused to come.

The sports world news from the night before was replaying and the ticker of scores was slowly scrolling along the bottom of the television screen.

"Jon, it's okay. Just tell somebody."

As if an announcer were speaking from the television, a voice, as clear and articulate as I've ever heard anything, spoke to me.

I turned my head to see if someone had entered the house. But no one was there. My heart began thumping, pounding like a drum. My breathing became quick and shallow, as though I were on the verge of hyperventilating. Someone had spoken directly to me.

As I concentrated on where the voice had come from, my body felt an overwhelming rush of calmness and peace. The tears quickly dried up and a sense of hope began to settle in my heart. It was as if arms had wrapped around me and were holding me like a mother holds her newborn baby. I felt safe and secure. And then the gentle, trusting voice spoke again: *It's okay. Just tell somebody.*

Perhaps I had just heard the answer to what I'd been seeking all this time. But the thought of coming clean frightened me. I had hidden my true identity for too long, living a double life. What would people do if they knew the real me? By telling it all, I was putting myself in a position to get destroyed by their words and actions. But the pain was too much to bear alone and it had lasted for far too long. I decided to trust the voice.

Immediately, I picked up my phone, not caring that it was 2:30 in the morning.

Call your boss. The thought passed through my mind and I almost ignored it. My boss? Did this voice not understand what a bad idea that could be?

Call your boss.

I punched his number into my phone and held my breath, certain this call too would go to voicemail. The first ring sounded and I heard the click of someone answering.

"Jon, what's wrong?" Wes Weatherred said, sounding genuinely concerned.

The dam broke, and I sobbed into the phone. "I need help and I don't know what to do. I want to die."

"I'm on my way. It's going to take me about fifteen minutes. Just hold on, okay?"

He knew where I lived, so I opened the front door and returned to my recliner to wait.

He made it to my house in record time. "What's going on?" he said, as soon as he walked through the door.

"Wes, I need help. I can't stop drinking." I had done it. I had admitted my problem and had asked for help. Now it was out in the open.

He looked at me as if to say, *What do you mean? I didn't even know you drank.* Of course he didn't. No one did. After the episode at the Christmas party, I doubled up my efforts to hide it from everyone, especially everyone at work.

I looked at him and swallowed hard. There was no turning back. This would be the first time I'd ever come clean with any-body. "I have a drinking problem. I can't seem to stop. Once I drink some, I want more and more. It's like I can't get enough." I spilled it all. Every secret, every hurt, every heartache, every insecurity. I told him everything.

He spoke very few words, but listened intently. And the more I talked, the better I felt. I realized it wasn't so bad to confess. It was actually freeing. As the darkness began to turn into light, the load of deception and lies that had weighed me down lifted as I shared some of my darkest, deepest secrets. Resentment and regret I had been holding onto for years were laid bare and the fears and insecurities lessened. I had taken a leap of faith in being honest and completely vulnerable and, for the first time, it had turned out better than I had expected. I'd set aside my pride and stopped pretending, and it was okay.

Wes never judged me. He never acted disgusted or angry. He listened compassionately, and when I'd finally finished, he said simply, "Jon, we're going to get you help. It's going to be all right."

He stayed with me that night, and I went to sleep. The next morning when I woke up, I felt free, but embarrassed. Would he still treat me with compassion? Or now that he'd had some time to process what I'd admitted, would he judge me? I held my breath when I saw him.

"Jon, I've been thinking about what you told me last night."

Uh-oh, here it comes, I thought.

"I'm committed to getting you help." As soon as the words left his mouth, I felt my shoulders relax and untense themselves. "But I don't even know where to start here."

"Yeah," I said. "I don't either." So we went online and googled alcohol rehab centers. I called the first one that popped up, La Hacienda Treatment Center, in Hunt, Texas, about four hours from where I lived. But it was a residency program, where I'd have to go and stay onsite. I glanced at Wes, unsure if his help went as far as giving me that kind of time off work. But he nodded his approval.

La Hacienda had no beds available. "Let me do some checking and I'll call you back," the man there told me. "But we may not have anything for another week." I couldn't wait that long. I'd already confessed my troubles, now I needed desperately to move forward or I knew I'd put it off and end up back where the previous night had led me. So I went back to Google and began calling other rehab centers from the list. With each call, though, I felt more impressed that I was supposed to go to La Hacienda.

Okay, how do I go there if they have no beds? I argued with my heart.

Later that afternoon, I still hadn't found a rehab facility I felt comfortable with and I was getting irritable. "None of these feel right to me! What am I going to do?"

"It's okay, Jon," Wes told me, who was still there and committed to staying with me to see things through. "We'll find you the right place."

By 3:00 I still hadn't heard back from La Hacienda, and I was jittery and upset, so I called them again. I recognized the man's voice as the one with whom I'd spoken earlier.

"Just checking," I said, trying to sound calm. "Have you been able to find out anything? Any openings?"

"I'm sorry." He answered me with a caring tone. "Nothing yet, but I'll keep my eyes and ears open and let you know as soon as—"

"No! Please, you don't understand," I pled, unable to control my emotions. My tears were falling fast and free. "I need help *now*. I can't go another day."

It must have been my pleading, or perhaps he connected with something in my voice. In that same caring tone, he kindly said, "I do understand. I'm a recovering alcoholic. Let me call you back in fifteen minutes, okay?"

"Okay. Please, *please* help me if you can." My whole life I'd prided myself on being in control and doing things myself. I was so low, so desperate, so anguished, that all I could do was surrender and admit that I couldn't do this alone.

True to his word, fifteen minutes later the phone rang. "We have a place for you. Be here at 1:00 tomorrow and we'll check you in."

Relief swarmed around me and I smiled. "Thank you. Thank you!" *I have another chance*, I realized. *It isn't over for me yet.*

They had a bed for me. They wanted to help me get better. All I needed to do was pack some clothes and show up. Wes even offered to drive me there. Wes and I would leave early the next morning. When Wes saw I was no longer a threat to myself, he went home. "I'll see you tomorrow bright and early," he said. "Get a good night's sleep."

"Hey, Wes. Is it okay if I ask Shannon to come along?" I'd stayed with Shannon's mom for a few weeks while I was going through the divorce. He was my best friend and a coworker, and I thought he would provide an added level of strength and comfort for me.

"Of course."

I immediately called him to let him know what had happened. "Absolutely I'll come along, Jon," Shannon told me. "I'm glad you're getting help; I've been worried about you. And don't worry about your clients and work. I'll cover all of that for you."

Another sense of relief washed over me. I didn't have to worry about work.

I had one more person to tell. I picked up the phone once again, and this time I called Stephanie.

As soon as she said hello, I could tell she was surprised and hesitant about the call. I took a deep breath. I could do this. I had already confessed and it wasn't as terrible as I'd feared, so I could own up to Stephanie. But I was still afraid she would laugh or scoff or judge me. Still I knew I needed to face my own demons.

"Hey, I'm going to get help. I can't stop drinking," I told her.

When she spoke, her voice was filled with compassion and kindness. "Good. You need some help, Jon, and I'm glad you're doing this. And don't worry about the kids. They're in good hands, and when you get back, they'll be happy to see you."

The next morning I gathered up what I figured I'd need and got into Wes's car for the ride that I hoped would finally change my life. I was excited to move on, to get help, to start a different life. But once we pulled into the parking lot, I got scared. What if it didn't work? What if this was too hard? What were they going to do to me? It seemed as though all the alcohol demons sensed that they were going to lose hold on me and started clawing at my mind to make me fear this place.

"I don't want you to leave," I admitted to Wes and Shannon, on the verge of crying.

"It'll be okay, Jon," Wes said. "They're here to help you get better."

I grabbed my bags and pushed back my shoulders. It was time to face my fears. An older man in his mid-sixties, with gray hair and glasses, met me as soon as I entered the building. When he said hello, I knew this was the man I'd talked to over the phone. His eyes held a deep kindness and understanding. He seemed like the perfect grandpa-figure for me. He led me to my room, introducing me to people along the way. They all, too, seemed glad I was there and eager to see me succeed.

As soon as I walked through the doors that day, March 27, 2010, I realized I had nothing to be afraid of. I felt a sense of peace. When I saw other people who were going through what I experienced—and they seemed to be doing okay—I realized I wasn't alone. Somehow, throughout my life, I'd created this sense that nobody else in the world had the same problem as I did. But being in this place with others like me showed me that I *wasn't* the only one. They were getting help, and now I was too.

One of my greatest concerns was that people were going to judge me. They were going to think, *Ah, he's just a drunk. He's such a loser.* I was sure they would think that because that's what I'd think about people. I'd often thought, *People just can't handle their drink. Why don't they have some self-control?* But no one ever treated me that way. Instead they explained about alcoholism. They said, "This is a mental obsession, a physical craving, and a spiritual problem. We're going to really focus on the spiritual."

I'd gone to church, so I figured I already knew that part of it, but I was determined to follow whatever program they put me on, if it meant I could experience freedom from the miserable life I'd been living.

For the first few days they had me in detox where they monitored me. For a guy who believed I could quit any time I wanted, this was torture. I craved alcohol. *Just a sip*, I thought. *That's all I need. A tiny sip and I'll be fine.*

But I had to keep reminding myself that it was never just a sip. A sip was what led me to another and another and another until I was stone-cold drunk. "Just a sip" was what had landed me here!

For twenty-eight days I stayed at the rehab facility. My mind began to clear and I could think soberly again. They worked with me to help me see some of the root of my problems and failed expectations, how instead of facing them straight on and coping, I'd turned to alcohol, which only masked the problems, and ultimately, made them worse.

La Hacienda is based on the 12-Step program, which AA (Alcoholics Anonymous) also is based on. So I learned the importance of those steps and began to understand how powerful they are in my life.

I learned:

1. I am powerless over alcohol—that my life had become unmanageable.

2. A Power greater than myself could restore me to sanity.

3. I needed to turn my will and my life over to God's care as I understand him more.

4. I needed to make a searching and fearless moral inventory of myself.

5. I must admit to God, to myself, and to another person the exact nature of my wrongs.

6. I am entirely ready to have God remove all my character defects.

7. I can humbly ask him to remove my shortcomings.

8. I need to list everyone I've harmed and be willing to make amends with them—seeking their forgiveness.

9. Being willing isn't enough. I must actually make direct amends whenever I can, unless doing so would bring them more pain.

10. It's important to continue to take stock of myself and promptly admit when I'm wrong.

11. I must consciously meditate and pray for knowledge that will help me do what is right and then ask God for the power to follow through on that knowledge with action.

12. Continuing to grow and practice these principles for the rest of my life will allow me to mature and will give me the ability to help others who also struggle.

Those steps were tough to wade through and embrace, especially because so much of my life had been about me having control, me being right, me-me-me. But that kind of mentality and living had gotten me into this mess. I'd learned all too well that it couldn't help me get out of it.

Over the course of those twenty-eight days, I steeped myself in learning, understanding, and embracing those steps. I even purchased a Recovery Bible and began reading it. Growing up I'd never had any interest in reading the Bible. Mostly it didn't make sense to me. I didn't know how to read it. I'd read all those names and ancestries and stuff, and it was boring. But reading it now felt as if the blinders had been lifted from my mental eyes and I found peace and hope within its pages. The Recovery Bible specifically highlighted the 12-step program, so for each step it explained what the step was and why it was essential to experiencing freedom, and then it backed up the principle through highlighting Bible verses that focused specifically on each area. It grabbed my attention and interest, and I could relate to what it was say-ing. The Bible wasn't stale, it actually had deep insight and wisdom for my life.

As I grew in my understanding of those twelve steps, I was able to let go of my unmet expectations and my need to be right and to prove others wrong. I realized how far I had come when about half-way through the program, we had a family session in which Stephanie, my mother, brother, and sister-in-law participated. In a safe environment, for the first time they were able to share with me some of their hurts. And for the first time, I was able to hear them, really hear them, and not deflect or defend what I did to them. I was able to listen and not lash out at them, but simply acknowledge, "I did that. I was wrong."

It was the most humbling thing I'd ever done, but it was also freeing. I didn't have to fear or pretend to be somebody I wasn't. And my family accepted me, with no hesitation. I really started to experience forgiveness.

Forgiveness was not a concept I easily understood or practiced. To me, forgiveness had always been conditional and based on my expectations of how others were to behave. But they offered forgiveness freely and unconditionally, showing me love and compassion.

As the remnants of the all-day benders slowly escaped my body and I practiced getting healthy, the meaning of life began to change. My view was becoming brighter. With each hurt that was eliminated from my body, the more gentle and loving my thoughts became. Instead of anger and rage taking over, feelings of remorse for my part and my actions became present. With each story others shared with me, the softer and more tender my heart became, melting away the hard and calloused blisters. Instead of trying to fix others, I felt compassion and a genuine desire to help.

When my twenty-eight days were completed, I felt like a new man. A confidence resided in me, and I thought, *My life is going to be great. Everything is going to fall into place for me.*

The counselors' final gifts to me were to set me up with a counselor, Carole DeLongchamps, and to encourage me to connect with a local AA group, find a sponsor, and attend the meetings as faithfully as I could. That would be easy, I promised them. If those groups kept me feeling this great, I'd have no problem attending.

So I found a group about thirty minutes from my house, and the day after I returned home, I walked into the meeting. I was surrounded by sixty or so other like-minded/like-experienced people and I felt as if I'd found my tribe. As I listened to other people share, I thought, *These people are just like me.* I related to everything they said. I even discovered that some of them had done even crazier stunts than I had! *Man, I did some crazy stuff but I've never done something like that.* But I never judged them—and they never judged me. We were all together on this journey toward wholeness and freedom. Everyone was focused on reaching out and helping one another.

And Carole helped me recognize defense mechanisms, such as sarcasm and flippancy, within myself that I'd used to cope in various situations in which I felt threatened or insecure. She was a straight-shooter, and I respected her for that.

"Behind every sarcastic comment is fear," she would say to me.

As I considered her challenges to me, I realized she was right. I'd lived much of my life afraid and insecure. I feared not being good enough, blowing opportunities, not having money, nobody liking me. My list of fears went on and on. But she and my AA group helped me face my insecurities and fears to fight against them.

I was on a new journey. It was time to throw away the "victim card" and start working toward obtaining the status of "victor." Life was not that bad at all. And I was no longer going to allow alcohol to take me down that old path again. I was going to be different; I was going to be in control.

And I did well . . . until one day, four months after I was released from rehab, when I took just one more sip.

CHAPTER 20
AN AWFUL RELAPSE

I was furious. I'd recently learned someone close to me had betrayed me and now the thoughts of his betrayal consumed me. I struggled to concentrate at work, when I was out with friends or family, and especially when I was home alone with my thoughts.

It was August and I'd only been out of rehab four months.

I brought it up with my counselor, and as we worked through it, I slowly felt I was gaining freedom. But one morning while I was at work, for some reason, my resolve grew weak and all the pain and anger dropped back over me like a bomb.

I can't believe he did that to me, I kept thinking. *Why would he do that?* The more my thoughts dwelled on the past events, the angrier I became until I was ready to explode. I didn't want to forgive him—I wanted to get him back. I wanted to have it out with him. I wanted to hurt him the way I felt hurt.

I left my office and headed to my friend Shannon's desk. "I just want to kill him, I'm so angry at him," I told Shannon, who knew what had happened. As I worked myself up more into a frenzy, I thought, *A drink sure would make me feel better right now.* Immediately the craving roared back to life, after having hibernated for months. I thought about how vodka would loosen me up, help me forget how angry I was, and calm me down. Even though, I knew it wouldn't really calm me down—it would embolden me to confront the person whom I now viewed as my enemy.

"Screw it all, I'm getting drunk tonight!" I said. I knew I shouldn't have admitted that to Shannon, especially since he and Wes had driven me to rehab and he saw what a mess I had been. But I didn't care. I lost all sense of reason and propriety. *I just wanted a drink!*

Shannon grimaced at my announcement and shook his head slightly, but didn't say anything. He knew me well enough to understand that once I set my mind to something, nothing could change it—including a friend's well-intentioned words.

Because my job was in sales, it was easy for me to come and go from the office without any eyebrows raising, since most of my work included making sales calls offsite anyway, so I grabbed my briefcase and left the office around noon without anyone, besides Shannon, knowing my true intentions. I stopped at the liquor store by my house, bought a 1.75-liter bottle of Popov, and headed home. As soon as I walked through the door, I immediately headed to the kitchen, grabbed the largest cup I could find, and poured the vodka in, filling it to the brim.

I placed the drink in front of me and looked down at it for a moment. This would be the first time I'd been this close to a drink since that fateful drinking binge four months before. But now things were different. I really needed this drink. I could handle it, right? Yeah, I told myself confidently. One drink—not a big deal. Even though I knew I wouldn't stop at just one.

I thought about my counselor and my AA sponsor. What would they say if they knew what I was about to do? As my mind rationally tried to remind me of the twelve-steps and of how far I'd come and how well I'd done, I pushed those thoughts aside, replacing them with my justifications for drinking this bottle of vodka. "Yeah, I don't care anymore," I muttered out loud. Hey, it was either drink or kill somebody—I thought that was pretty righteous of me to choose the drinking option.

My hand grasped the thirty-two ounce Styrofoam cup. It cradled in perfectly, as if it were made just for me. I licked my lips, anticipating the sweet, calming taste.

The first sip was everything wonderful I had remembered. It went down smoothly.

Ah, this is good.

I took a gulp next. *Why bother with just sipping*? I told myself. The effects of the drink settled in and I felt really good. That sense of confidence returned, and I enjoyed my second drink.

The second one turned into the third and fourth, and before I knew it, the bottle was almost empty.

By early evening I heard a knock at my door.

"Hey, Jon, I just wanted to check up on you," Shannon said as he came in. I was glad to see him; it gave me an audience for my rants and ramblings. For the next several hours, as I continued to drink, I went from rage to tears and back again. I wanted peace so badly, but no matter how much I drank or ranted, I couldn't make peace come.

In rehab I learned that alcoholism is progressive. It sinks you deeper and deeper and does it faster and faster with each relapse. That one decision to drink for that night put me in the express lane. I was full on drinking. After that night, I drank. And drank. And drank. I didn't let even one opportunity pass by. I drank worse than I had before. By now, I pitched out the Diet Coke and drank the vodka straight up. I was downing almost a half-gallon of it a day. But I continued to attend AA meetings, sometimes going drunk. I would listen to the others and how they had successfully beaten the disease and I'd think, *I can't do this. I can't get sober. I just can't.*

As if my sponsor and the rest of the group knew exactly what I was going through, they'd say to me, "You *can* do this, Jon. You can."

I didn't believe them, but I continued to show up at the meetings as well as with my therapy sessions with Carole. One day after we discussed the struggles I was having and how they were all coming back and haunting me, she suggested that I consider reentering a rehab center. She reminded me that I couldn't change the circumstances of the betrayal or my divorce or my lost dreams and I couldn't force the other person to acknowledge or apologize for what he had done to me. I needed to focus on what I *could* control, which was me—my thoughts, my actions, my ability to forgive and move forward. "For your fortieth birthday," she said, "you need to give yourself a gift and go to rehab." She suggested that I go to Willingway Hospital in Statesboro, Georgia.

I told her I would, but once I was out of her office and back to my daily routines, I shoved her suggestion to the back of my mind. As my birthday approached, I still hadn't contacted Willingway; instead I focused on what I now did best—drink. But once again, the alcohol only temporarily eased my shame and guilt and insecurities. I had a habit of calling people when I got so drunk that the alcohol failed to help me forget. I'd always cry and talk about how much I hated myself and how I wished I were dead. A week or so before my birthday, at around midnight, I called Carole.

"I want to die," I cried over the phone.

"Jon, call Willingway. Do it now."

I did. But when somebody answered, I went into a rage. I yelled at how I wanted to kill myself and how I was going crazy.

The nurse tried to calm me down. "We'll have a bed ready for you immediately. Please just come as soon as you can."

It took me a few more days before I knew I needed to go. I thought about how much I'd messed up my life—a common thought recurrence. I could have been a great baseball player. I could have been a great coach. I could have been a great husband and father. I could have been a multi-millionaire. I could have been . . . I could have . . . I could have . . .

I was ready to go. But this time, I was finished playing around. I didn't want to get better, relapse, hate myself, get better, and do it all over again. I didn't want to keep on the never-ending rollercoaster of trouble.

The day before I left for Georgia, which also happened to be the day before my birthday, I walked into my boss's office, unsure if he was going to be as supportive this time around. "Wes, I don't know if I'm going to have a job when I come back, but I've got to go again."

"You got to do what's best for you," he said. "Don't worry. You'll have a job when you get back."

And Shannon stepped up again and assured me that he'd handle my clients and work. He also offered to drive me to the airport. The next day, September 7, 2010, I flew to Georgia.

Willingway was similar to La Hacienda in that it was based on the 12-step program. The counselor assigned to me was a straight-shooting, no holds-barred, tough guy named Raymond, who took none of my guff and challenged every argument and excuse I had with pointing out how *I* had made all the choices in my life, and then he'd follow up with, "How do you know that wasn't God's plan?"

I wasn't all that interested in bringing God into my rehab. He hadn't been all that helpful before, I figured. Even though I did have to admit it was probably God's voice I heard the night of my binge in which he said, "Tell somebody." But other than that, what good had he brought into my life?

"Jon Peters, you're crazy, bro," he'd say. "You know you chose to do those things. You try to blame everybody for everything. Why don't you take some responsibility?" I hated hearing him say those things to me. I hated feeling like he was holding up a mirror to me and forcing me to look at my true reflection. I didn't like what I saw. But he wouldn't allow a pity party. "You want to get better? Open up the big book."

So we'd open the Alcoholics Anonymous book. "Turn to this page and read what it says," he'd say.

So I would turn to the page and read about how I should fix my problem. "Page 87, last paragraph, first sentence: As we go through the day we pause, when agitated or doubtful, and ask for the right thought or action." I'd look up at Raymond. "Ooh, yeah, that would work. You're right," I'd have to admit.

Or he'd tell me to look up page 84, the last paragraph, the first two sentences. "Read it out loud."

"And we have ceased fighting anything or anyone—even alcohol. For by this time sanity will have returned."

"Why don't you start trusting God and try some of this?"

Despite myself, I started to agree with what Raymond was saying about me. I did make choices. I did have a lot more power than I liked to give myself credit for. And I did find help and strength through the big book of Alcoholics Anonymous, but more importantly, through the Bible. It was as though I got addicted to working on myself. It became a challenge, and just as in baseball when I'd committed to doing whatever it took to be better, I transferred that desire into working on myself. I realized that living was very similar to playing baseball. If I wanted to perform well on the baseball field, I had to spend quality time in practice. The same held true for life. Nothing of greatness comes easy; it all takes work. With the same intensity and focus I had given to baseball, I was now preparing to live life. Not on my terms—that had not worked. But on life's terms. I was learning to adjust to the nuances of life but, more importantly, I was learning more about myself. I knew myself inside and out, but the years of hiding and pretending had influenced who I had become. I needed reprogramming updates to complete the overhaul. If you do something consistently for a period of time, you eventually become a creature of habit. I had become a monster. But that was changing.

Each morning I'd wake up feeling good and I started to see real results of my hard work. Things that used to make me mad didn't make me mad anymore. I felt more peaceful, happier, more at ease in my own skin.

Toward the end of my twenty-eight days there, Raymond gave me an assignment. "I want you to write a letter to your old self." He didn't want me to write a "hey, Jon, you're okay" kind of letter, but a deep, raw, honest confrontation that I would have with myself. It was one of the hardest things I'd ever done. That night I sat in my room, pen in hand, and stared down at the pad of blank paper.

I began to list all the things I had done, all the pain I'd caused—both myself and others—from as far back as I could remember. As the words fell onto the page, I couldn't believe I had become this kind of person, because deep down I knew that really wasn't who I was in my heart or who I wanted to be. I didn't want that person to have any part of me any longer.

Page after page I poured out the confessions and truth. After several hours I was spent. The letter was finished.

The next morning, I took the letter and met with Raymond outside by a fire pit.

"I'd like you to read the letter out loud," he said.

I cringed. It was bad enough writing it and reading it silently. Now I had to utter my sins for the world to hear.

With each sentence, my eyes grew thick with the accumulated tears of years of pain. I wiped at them, only to have them fill up again. I stuttered and stumbled through the letter, crying and wiping tears away, so ashamed of what I had become.

Finally I finished and kept my head down, my weary eyes averted from Raymond's gaze.

He told me to place the letter in the middle of the fire pit, then he handed me some matches. "Jon, it's time to let it all go. It's time to let the past be in the past, to leave it there, and to look forward to a new future."

I struck the match and threw it, burning brightly, onto my letter. It poofed with a speck of smoke and then began burning the pages.

Raymond didn't say anything, but as we watched the pages disappear, he grabbed me in a tight embrace, as if to say, *Jon, just feel this. Feel your feelings. It's okay.*

The burning letter was releasing me from my past. I didn't have to be held captive by it any longer. I was safe and secure here, but when I returned to Houston and my life, could I still release the past and completely let it go? Could I be strong enough not to relapse again? Could life really and truly be different this time around?

CHAPTER 21
MEETING GOD

"How do you know that wasn't God's plan?"

Raymond's question continued to nag at me. I was back home, faithfully attending AA meetings, and going more regularly to church, but I was still struggling with the whole God thing. How did I know that doing so well in baseball and then having to give up that dream wasn't part of God's bigger plan for me? How did I know that marrying Stephanie and her having two babies wasn't part of God's bigger plan? How did I know that entering rehab and getting help wasn't part of God's bigger plan? The truth was, I didn't know any of it.

I'd listen to people talk about God and who he was to them, yet I didn't have a clear understanding of who he was in my life. I had so many images of him from my childhood and my mother's faith. Her beliefs had always been very strong, but they were her beliefs. If I were going to believe in God or even know who he was, I couldn't just cling to my mother's faith—or to anybody else's. I had to experience God and know he was real in *my* life. I could remember moments in church when I felt a presence that was strong and that grabbed my heart. Those moments always made me feel joyful. Was that what faith was?

I began asking myself the tough but real questions. What is my purpose? Why am I here? What am I supposed to do? What is this all about? But the questions never seemed to provide any real answers. Could they have some connection to God?

I thought I believed in God—I *said* I believed in him but it was all "mouth service." Was he the missing link? I always knew there had to be more to life, and that I was missing something. I tried for a long time to figure out religion. I had a hard time doing something without knowing the *why*. I just couldn't get my head around the why having anything to do with faith or God.

A few months after I left Willingway, in late January 2011, my friend, John Harrison, invited me to a men's weekend retreat called the Journey to Damascus. He said he would be my sponsor there.

When I asked him to tell me exactly what it was, he responded, "I think you'll benefit from the experience. Don't worry about it. You'll see."

I didn't take that as a good sign, but I trusted John. He had a lot of wisdom and he often helped me out by allowing me to talk through my struggles. And he was a strong believer in God, which made me fascinated by his faith. He was so confident and settled in who he was and he never made me feel as though I was inferior to him or as though I was a bad person. I also remembered what my therapist, Carole, had taught me: "Jon, just do three things. I want you to be honest, I want you to be open-minded, and I want you to be willing." So I agreed to go.

Usually before I went anywhere, I'd check out what I was getting myself into. But he believed this Journey to Damascus would help me in my life, so I decided simply to trust him and go into it blind.

One cold Friday night we drove the hour together to the retreat center, which was nestled on about forty-five acres in a country campground and lake setting with lots of trees and walking paths. The place was beautifully landscaped and well-kept. The center consisted of a chapel, a main conference building, a dining "chow" hall, and cabins spread throughout the property.

That night we met the other men, there were about a hundred in attendance, got our cabin lodging assignments, and attended a worship service in the main building. As I sat in the service, I knew coming to this "journey" was a big mistake.

The leaders explained that the Journey to Damascus was to help strengthen our foundations in Christ and to foster unity with other believers. The weekend would be about building faith and community. I was okay with that—it was fairly typical Christian retreat stuff. They told us one of the best ways to do that was to completely unplug—no cell phones, no work. And then the leaders called us "pilgrims."

Yeah, that's a bit much, I thought.

Then a three-to-four-member band got on the stage and led us in worship music. Many of the men throughout the room were clapping and smiling.

This isn't for me, I thought, crossing my arms and refusing to participate. *What a bunch of fakers. Nobody is this free and happy.* I was skeptical of people who "over praised" and danced and raised their hands. The room was filled with them. *This is ridiculous! What hypocrites!* I felt on the verge of picking up my stuff, finding John, and saying, "Get me out of here. I am done!"

That was always my MO. But I clinched my teeth as I remembered that I promised myself to take it all in and experience the whole weekend. I only hoped that the next two days would be over before I knew it.

After the service, they gave us instructions to go to our cabins and not talk to anyone. We were to spend the rest of the evening in silence, contemplating our time there and listening to see what God had in store for us.

This is like some cult! What did John get me into? If anyone tries to make me do something I don't want to do, they better watch out. I felt prepared to fight. I didn't know if they were going to try some kind of ridiculous initiation "hazing" stuff or what.

Well, I had no problem with the not talking to anybody part. I was in a cabin with several other men, none of whom I knew—or wanted to get to know. Fortunately, now I wouldn't have to. The cabin had a living room in the middle and a bedroom off to the right and to the left. I took my things into the room to the left and spent the night stewing over why I was there and what I was supposed to "hear" from God. All I heard was the wind outside and an occasional cricket or bullfrog.

The next morning after breakfast, the leaders divided everyone into groups. These assigned groups were to stick together for the entire weekend. Each group sat at a table and each table had a leader who was there to facilitate discussions. We then listened to speakers on different topics, such as grace, the priesthood of all believers, priorities, discipleship, Christian action. Each speaker shared a piece of his story and discussed what the Bible had to say about the topic. Then the groups would talk about it among themselves.

I wasn't really "feeling" this set-up, although I did resonate with a few of the speakers who shared about some of the struggles they'd experienced—alcohol, drugs, failed marriages. In one session we talked about marriage and relationships. I ached as I listened to the speaker highlight the important role husbands and fathers play in their families. It was just another stab to my already fragile and insecure ego, only made worse by a guy in my group named Tom. Tom was an older gentleman, probably in his late sixties, who was nicely dressed, professional looking, and carried himself with a sense of confidence. Whenever he answered questions or contributed to the discussion, he was well-spoken and articulate. I thought he was more of a smooth talker, which made me skeptical of him. He struck me as a little too polished, a little too "all put together." He had been married for decades. When I mentioned at the table that I was no longer married, he said, "Behind every good man is a good woman." When I would answer other questions, I tried to be honest—"Yeah,

I've failed to put my family first at times when I'd rather be drinking or partying with my friends." And always he felt the need to respond. "Oh my. Really? Wow!" While everyone else seemed supportive, I felt he was more interested in shaming me. Behind his glances and comments, I really felt as he were saying, "I can't believe you did that. Shame on you!"

I felt judged and scolded. He reminded me of my past and kept telling me what I "needed." Finally after listening to his jabs through multiple topics and hours, I could take no more. "Tom, you don't know what I need," I said, calling him out. But what I really wanted to say was, "Shut up, man! You don't know anything about me. I could not care less about what you have to say."

At least he calmed down after that, but I was already wound up and ticked off. So of course, what better to follow than for all of us to start singing again. I *hated* it.

Come on, Jon, just be open-minded. I heard Carole's mantra in my brain. That was easy for her to say; she wasn't there with me.

We had some free time in which I took a walk alone and then we were all back together Saturday evening for another session. The sun was starting to set and the leaders took us to a chapel on the other side of the retreat center. As each of us entered the chapel, we received a packet along with instructions for what to do with it. I sat off by myself at the back and opened the manila envelope. Inside were a dozen or so letters. John, who was my sponsor for the retreat, had asked some friends to write letters to me.

Each letter talked to me about what a good friend I was, how I was a good guy with a good heart, and how fortunate my friends were to have me in their lives. It was difficult to stay in a bad mood reading such uplifting comments.

What's this about? I wondered. I still couldn't understand why John felt it was so important for me to be at this retreat or what I was supposed to get out of it. Another thought drifted through my mind, *Just stick it out. Who knows what's going to happen?*

Even though everyone began to fill up the chapel, no one spoke. We were supposed to stay open to hearing God's whispers to us. It still felt weird—this intentional silence. The wind had picked up outside and was howling. I looked back over the letters and wondered again why I was here. What was the point?

An older man in his seventies stood in front of us. He was short and plump. With a soft and sweet voice, he introduced himself as Pastor Carl and told us he would be leading the evening's session. He talked about the importance of resting in God, how we needed to learn to let go of our worries, stress, pain, and hurts, and just be present with God. That we could trust him with all those things that keep us from experiencing true rest.

"I'd like you to picture a very beautiful place," Pastor Carl said. "Close your eyes and get that image in your mind." Someone started playing the piano softly in the background.

Okay, this is Looney Tunes stuff. What are we doing? I glanced around the room to see everyone shutting their eyes. I didn't want to be the only guy who refused to cooperate, so I shut them, still thinking about how crazy this all was. *Okay, some place beautiful.*

I couldn't envision anything and felt frustrated. But soon I let my mind wander, and I remembered my honeymoon in Hawaii. *That was beautiful*, I thought. I began to get an image of the landscape where Stephanie and I got married. It was in a curve of the land at the top of a cliff that looked out over lush green scenery of a golf course against the mountainside on the other side of the curve with the ocean coming in the middle. About ten feet or so from where Stephanie and I were married was a cliff that dropped down into the bluest-blue ocean. I pictured the waves coming into a nearby beach on the other side of the curve, but instead of crashing in, they were coming in slow and smooth with little whitecaps to them. I was standing at the cliff, looking out over the beautiful landscape. It was amazing to recall.

After a few moments Pastor Carl spoke again. "Now in this beautiful setting, picture you and Jesus together."

I gasped. I turned slightly in my mind and watched Jesus appear from behind the edge of the cliff and walk toward me. *"Hey, Jon, take a leap,"* he said. *"Take a leap. I promise I've got you. I'll catch you."* He smiled as he walked toward me. A peace settled on me like I've never experienced before. It was as if in Jesus' presence I had no problems, no pain, no shame, no guilt, just total love and acceptance. The image was so real, I felt like I'd actually transported myself to that spot in Hawaii and Jesus was actually, literally standing right in front of me with his arms wide open.

You're real, I thought.

He smiled again.

As Pastor Carl led us to end that time of contemplation, I watched Jesus walk back away from the cliff where I could no longer see him. My chest grew heavy and I felt panicked. *"Where are you?"* I called out to him. *"Don't leave me! Come back. Please?"*

In that instant I felt as if someone had turned off the old light bulb in my brain and replaced it with a new one. I *knew* God was real. I knew he had a hand in my life. I knew he was the key to meaning and my life's purpose. I knew he was the one who could completely wipe away all of my failures and mistakes and hurts and fill me with his peace and wholeness.

"God, forgive me. Forgive me for all the ways I've failed you and rebelled against you. I want to live for you, Jesus!" In that instant I took a leap, giving my life completely to God, knowing without a doubt that he would be there to catch me. I was different; I was changed. And when it came time to sing again, tears of joy streamed down my face and I was clapping and smiling along with everybody else. God had saved me.

CHAPTER 22
A NEW DREAM

"Man, whatever happened to you, it was like you were on fire," John told me on the way home from the retreat. "I had a feeling something was going to happen, but I didn't know what."

I knew what it was. God had finally gotten a hold of my life because I had finally listened and let him. Now I couldn't get enough of God.

All the pain, guilt, and shame—gone. My anger—gone. All my cravings—gone. No relapses. Total healing and restoration, and he placed within my spirit a deep, profound joy. The Bible says that God will repay us for the years the locusts have eaten (see Joel 2:25). He has. And he continues to redeem and restore my life. God used the loss of baseball and my dreams and he used my drinking and AA to help me find a true and meaningful life.

The retreat leaders had encouraged us to begin journaling so we could see God's hand at work in our lives and in the lives of those around us. It would help us remember what we had experienced and how faithful God is to us. I took their encouragement to heart and every morning I woke up before the sun rose, read my Bible, prayed—a new experience for me, to be sure!—and journaled. My outlook turned positive, as if I knew something good was about to happen each day, and so I focused my eyes on looking for that good thing. God never disappointed me. It was amazing that when I began to look for good things, I found them everywhere! Every day I would list all the things I could be grateful for that day. Then I also used my journal to record my prayer requests.

For instance, I began to pray for a buddy of mine who was struggling with his drinking, so I journaled my prayers for him that he would reach out for recovery. I knew God would answer my prayers, I just waited to see how. Later that *same day*, my phone rang. It was him.

"Hey, Jon, can you come pick me up?"

"Sure, where are we going?"

"I need some help with my drinking. I've booked a plane ticket to Willingway. Can you take me to the airport?"

I laughed. *That's just God working*, I thought. *That's another answered prayer*. I used to see all those things as coincidences, but now I know there is no such thing. They're all God-winks! It's God saying, *I've got your back here. Trust me.* So I record all those in my journal, and when I go back periodically and reread what I've written, my faith increases.

I continue to practice journaling to this day.

Life seems to take on a journey of its own sometimes. You think you have it all figured out with nothing to worry about. And then, out of the blue, life throws you a curveball that leaves you standing at home plate with the bat on your shoulder. You are expecting a fastball and the pitcher surprises you with a breaking pitch. That's what had happened to me. I broke records and became a celebrity. I had the perfect girlfriend and high school baseball career. I had the best wife and family and job. I did all these great things, and yet I was still empty inside. I had tried almost everything to find my way in this world. I was an insider living in prison with an outsider's view. Although my future appeared to be bright, I was striking out at bat every time.

God finally got my attention, though. I'm grateful I listened to God that night in March 2010 when he told me to reach out and tell somebody, and I did. I took action. My *personal* relationship with him had begun. He placed me on a path toward finding him and filling the emptiness. He filled that emptiness and loneliness with himself. My hard, calloused heart was transformed into one that is softer, more compassionate, and filled with love.

The Bible explains the transformation: "If anyone is in Christ, the new creation has come: The old has gone, the new is here!" (2 Corinthians 5:17).

Each new day is an opportunity to start afresh. What we focus on is our choice. We all make mistakes and do things we wish could be different. Choosing to hang on to regrets, guilt, shame, and resentment only lead down a dark, gloomy, and destructive road. Adopting love, forgiveness, and acceptance can change our hearts. And it can change others.

At the end of the day, we have one question we must answer: What is it that truly matters? The answer is up to you. Is it all about you or is life really about the One who gives us life? That answer can make all the difference.

In a moment of utter despair that had been building for years and years, I found exactly what I had been searching for. It didn't come from a bottle. It didn't come from a person. It didn't come from success or money or any material possession. And it didn't come from baseball. It came directly from God. And there was nothing required of me other than my acceptance. It had seemed so difficult to do but it turned out to be so easy. It was—and is—the best thing that has ever happened to me.

Today, things have changed a lot in my life. I laugh a lot. I smile a lot. I cry a lot. I talk and forgive and love and pray a lot. And of course, I play around a lot. Some things never change, but over time and with action, some do. I am blessed and I have a lot to be grateful for. The *doom-and-gloom* outlook that had once been my constant companion has been replaced with a much more positive and uplifting one.

The fear I used to have about being a failure as a dad is gone. I know I still mess up at times, but I'm quick to ask my children for forgiveness and they're good to extend it. I tell them all the time that I love them and we have a great relationship. They're awesome children and I can't imagine my life without them in it.

Most important I love that I get to share who God really is with them. One day, about four years into my sobriety, I was taking my daughter, Kylie, to a swim meet. She sat silently in the back seat, which was unusual for her to be that quiet.

"You okay?" I asked.

"I'm nervous."

I felt for her because I remembered what that feeling before a competition was like. "Yeah, I know," I told her. "You'll do great. Do you know what you could do to make you feel better?"

She shook her head. "No."

"When I played baseball, I always got nervous before the game and I didn't know really what to do. But now when I get scared or fearful, I ask God to take it away, and it seems like he always does."

She looked at me in the rearview mirror, nodded, and appeared to ask God to take it from her.

Several months later at a swim meet, I asked her, "How are you? Nervous?"

"Yes," she said. Then she half-heartedly smiled. "But I've already asked God to take it away."

My heart melted! To think I could have missed that had I not sobered up and taken that leap into God's arms.

I used to make decisions in an instant but now when I am unclear on what to do, I pause, pray, and think about what the right thing to do is. I don't always do it but the majority of the time I do. Things do not always go my way. They never have and they never will. And that's okay with me now. There are some things I can control, but not many. While I was unable to put my marriage back together, Stephanie and I have reconciled and consider ourselves friends now. I admire and respect her as she is—a woman who has a huge servant's heart and a great mom. I've sought her forgiveness, she's offered it, and we work hard to make sure our kids know we love them unconditionally. I'm pleased when she smiles and tells me, "Wow, Jon, you really have changed!"

Today, instead of looking for the bad, I try to look for the good. I remind myself to "go on a praise hunt, not a sin hunt" and "it's not about me, it's about God." As long as I am God-centered, he can use me to be of maximum service to him and to others. I have learned that when I focus on controlling and changing the things I can and surrendering the things I cannot, life is very plentiful—plentiful with peace, joy, and freedom. That was hard for me to learn, but once I did, it became a normal way of life. I don't get it right all the time, and sometimes it's easier said than done. But it's about progress, not perfection.

I still get "fired up" at times and say and do things I shouldn't. Shutting my mouth when it's best to say nothing at all is still challenging for me. But now when I say or do something inappropriate, I take ownership for my actions and clean up my side of the street.

I still care about what others think of me and what they say about me—that hasn't changed. But what has changed is that I am more confident in who I am and I know my value. There is only one whose approval I am seeking, and that is God's. God thinks I am incredible. He thinks the same about you.

I pray continually throughout the day. It's important to me to have a quiet time to communicate with God. It may be for a few seconds or it may be for hours; either way, that time gets me centered on what is important and helps me focus on others. Being Jon-centered does not help me grow and it takes me away from serving and helping people. Getting out of myself is when I find life the most rewarding.

Jesus said, "If you ask, you will receive, and if you seek, you will find." I have experienced that. God's plans are good for us—that's his promise. And to keep it simple, there are really only two things he asks us to do: trust and obey.

Deep down inside all of us is a strong and overwhelming desire to do something significant, something that matters. For many of us, it consumes every thought and every action. It reflects what's important to us and who we are. Often it centers around our skills, talents, and abilities, and encourages and motivates us to be more than who we are—to be the best.

But what happens when the dreams are squashed? When our imagination that once brought so much excitement and energy begins to cripple us with doubts and insecurities? When our dreams become a distant memory of what we thought could really be true and could really happen?

For a long time, my dream was so true, so vivid, so real. I could see it, taste it, feel it, hear it, and smell it. It was me—all of me. It gave me a sense of purpose and a sense of satisfaction, motivating me to perform with excellence. Perhaps your dream, like mine, came naturally. You were in your element. No one was stopping you from your mission, and you were ready and willing to do whatever it took to make the dream a reality.

Many people will put all their hopes on a dream and don't know how to cope when they lose that dream. One day, something happens. They hesitate. They reconsider. They stop. And for one reason or another, they give up and are left holding a bag of empty dreams that once was fulfilling and gratifying. In an instant, the dreams vanish, leaving a gloomy, negative outlook.

I understand that all too well. My dreams were good, but baseball let me down. It wasn't a god I could depend on. No dreams are. But the Dream *Giver* is.

I don't regret my past or the loss of my baseball dreams; those things have taught me a lot and God has used them in amazing ways to help others. It's fun to look back and see how God blessed me with those opportunities and experiences. My record of fifty-three wins still stands. And every once in a while I still receive someone's old copy of *Sports Illustrated* with my photo on the cover and a request for me to sign it. Those things are fun to reminisce over, but ultimately, they don't complete or fulfill me.

God wastes nothing in our lives—not even dead dreams. I think throughout my baseball experiences God was preparing me to do something. I didn't go through all the baseball experiences and wasn't on the cover of *Sports Illustrated* or wasn't a national record holder just to let that fly away. There's a reason I went through that. I may never know completely his reasons and plan, but God does. So I continue to trust and obey, and God fills me with joy that never fades.

I'm so grateful God never gave up on me. When I surrendered my own will to him, I found he had been right there carrying me all along. He has washed me "white as snow" and has rendered me flawless.

He wants to do the same for you.

I have a new Coach and he has made all the difference. Happiness—abundant peace, enduring joy, and everlasting freedom. Isn't that what life's dreams are really all about?

AUTHOR'S NOTE

Have you ever wanted to do something but for one reason or another, you failed to take action? You never start. You discard whatever it may be and simply move on to the next idea. But one day in time, it recurs and becomes a thought that will not go away. And failing to do anything will no longer work. You must take action or else the mental obsession will take over.

That is exactly how I felt when I began this writing journey. Since late 2014, a "tug" of my heart was leading me to do more with my God-given talents, skills, and abilities. It was as though God was nudging and prodding me to share my life experiences with others, specifically the parts that I had carefully hidden—and to share in a real, genuine, and authentic way.

Because of my fear of rejection and what others would say about me, I wrestled with the idea of telling it all—the good, the bad, and the ugly. The fact that I felt less than and not good enough for the majority of my life was reason enough to delay and postpone. But as I stayed in my comfort zone, "sitting on the fence" and doing nothing, the "tug" of my heart became stronger and stronger. I had to act.

I often questioned, *What is this "tug" really about? Why is it getting stronger the more I ignore it? Why is it not going away? Is this just my mind fooling me and leading me once again in the wrong direction?*

I began asking God to show me exactly what *he* wanted me to do and for *him* to give me *his* courage to walk through any door *he* opened. I asked that he would help me see what *he* wanted me to see, hear what *he* wanted me to hear, feel what *he* wanted me to feel, and say whatever *he* wanted me to say. I reached out to men and women I admired and respected, seeking advice and wisdom in gaining clarity.

It has been a long road but one that has been well worth the distance. And finally, here it is—book completed!

The passion of my heart has always been about helping others and making a difference in someone's life. *Is there not a better way than to share my story?* My experiences are of no good to others if I keep them bottled up inside me. And perhaps something I have been through will help someone in some way or provide the encouragement to take that next step or keep going for one more day.

Whatever you've experienced, you aren't alone. God can change lives. No one is beyond his reach. And that's call for hope.

Not long ago, East Texas Baptist University contacted me to come and speak to the student body there. Since Coach Driggers had coached there previously, I called him that evening. Before we hung up, his last words to me were, "Jon, just keep answering the call." About ten minutes after that, my phone rang and it was a good friend. She said, "Hey, talk to me about this Jesus thing."

"What do you mean?"

"All my friends who are happy always talk about Jesus, and I need to know something about Jesus." So we talked and she said, "I don't know if I can grasp this."

"Just stay open-minded. Just keep seeking."

When I got off the phone, I thought about Coach Driggers' prophetic words: *Keep answering the call.* And so I do.

My story is just that—my story. It is no more important or more significant than yours. When we share our experiences, we stand a chance to gain understanding and to personally grow from hearing them. So I share. You can take my advice for what it's worth, or leave it—it's completely your choice. Perhaps you are walking back to the dugout, with the bat on your shoulder because you just struck out. Or maybe you have just hit a grand slam. Regardless of where you are now, there will come a time when the monkey will be on your back, clawing its way through the surface of your skin, causing you to feel like your world is crashing down, coming to an end. At that moment, you will need a solution. You will have to do something to get rid of the pain and the suffering. What will you do?

If you choose to come to the park, sit in the grandstands, and just watch the game, that's okay. Make sure you get some peanuts and Cracker Jacks. But if you want your name in the starting lineup and a chance to make the All-Star team, come down on the field and get ready to play. You are about to participate in the most exciting game of your life. Put on your hat and batting gloves, strap up your shoes, tighten your belt, and grab your glove and your bat. It's not going to be easy—nothing of greatness is. But it's going to be worth it. You and I—we are in this together. And there's no better time to blast off than right now. Are you ready to play ball?

Finally, this is the most important piece I can share with you: God loves you, and I love you. And there's nothing you can do about that! You can't stop him from loving you and desiring a *new* dream for your life—*his* dream. And that's the best dream ever.

DISCUSSION QUESTIONS

Feel free to use these discussion questions as reflections to help guide you to pursue your calling, passion, and faith journey, as journal starters for your own use, or as discussion starters in your small group or book study group.

If discussing in a group setting, feel free to be as open as you feel comfortable, with the goal of moving everyone toward more vulnerable and safe sharing. Remember these questions are not meant to bring judgment or guilt, but to help you gauge where you need to grow and experience freedom.

1. Ever since I was six years old, my dream was to be a professional baseball pitcher. I ate, breathed, and slept baseball.

   * What was your childhood dream? Why?
   * Describe your obsession with that dream.
   * What were your thoughts as it consumed you?
   * Did you chase after that dream?
   * If so, what did you do?
   * If not, why? What stopped you? What got in your way?
   * Do you still think about it today?

* Did your dream come true?
* If you were to die tomorrow, would you say, "I wished I would have done *that*?" What is *that*?
* Are you living your dream or someone else's?

2. Each of us has unique abilities, skills, and talents. When we use those specific qualities, we typically excel and thrive in whatever we choose to do. Many times, we find our purpose.

   * What are you good at? What abilities, skills, and talents do you possess?
   * Are you using them today?
   * If so, what results are you getting?
   * How do feel when you use them?
   * How do they make others feel?
   * If you aren't using them, why not?
   * What would it take for you to begin to use them? What is a good first step?
   * What's your purpose?

3. Think of a time when you "had it all." Life was good—you were content and filled with joy, peace, and freedom.

   * Describe that time.
   * Why was life so good?
   * What were you doing?
   * What did it feel like? Look like?
   * Who was in your life?

4. Think of the lowest time of your life, when you felt like you could not go on any longer. Nothing seemed to go your way. You wanted it to end—just to escape from reality. Perhaps you even wanted to die.

   * Describe that time.
   * What was happening at that point?

* What were you feeling?
* Why were you so low?
* What did you do about it?
* What were the results?
* Looking back, did you experience any personal growth?
* What lessons did you learn?

5. It has been said that we are only as sick as our deepest, darkest secrets. Think of a time when you pretended to "have it all." People around you thought everything was fine in your life. You showed your "fake smile" and your "fake happy personality" but deep down, you were feeling the exact opposite.

   * What secrets were/are you hiding?
   * Describe how they have affected you. Did they haunt you? Change your mood?
   * Why did you not want to reveal to someone what was really going on?
   * Did you eventually tell someone?
   * How long did you carry the burden?
   * When you finally confessed, how did it make you feel? What did that person or persons do?
   * If you're still clinging to those secrets, why? Would you be willing to take a risk and confess?

6. Generosity is often thought of in terms of giving money. I prefer to define generosity as more of an intrinsic, heartfelt action in which you give 100 percent of yourself, 100 percent of the time.

   * What does the word *generosity* mean to you?
   * Who is the most generous person in your life?
   * Why would you consider them generous?
   * What have they done for you?
   * How did they make you feel?

* Are you generous?
* When have you shown someone generosity? And why?
* What did you do?
* How did your actions make you feel?

7. We are all broken in some form or fashion. We are not perfect by any means. But to take no action to change by resting on those statements is only an excuse. Time and time again I have witnessed people change for the better.

   * Do you believe you can change?
   * What are three of your character flaws?
   * How do they impede your personal growth?
   * How do they affect your relationships? Your work? Your daily activities?
   * Have others noticed and mentioned them? If so, what have they said?
   * What's the root of the flaws?
   * What can you do to recognize and eliminate them?

8. It takes just a small amount of hope to keep going.

   * If someone came to you seeking help because they lost hope, what would you tell them?
   * How would you encourage them?
   * Have you ever lost hope?
   * What pulled you through that tough time?

9. Defining moments are times when something happens that has a profound effect on us. It could be good or bad. They usually cause us to change, and they stay with us for a while, sometimes our whole lives.

   * What are two defining moments in your life?
   * What specifically happened? Was it good? Bad?
   * Who was involved?

* In what ways did it change you?
* Describe your feelings then and now.
* Have your feelings changed over time? If so, in what ways?

10. I have been given many chances in life. Regardless of the many things I have done and said that were wrong, people never gave up on me.

* Who has always believed in you?
* Who is that person you can count on to support you no matter what?
* How do they make you feel?
* What qualities come to mind when you think of that person?
* What is it that you have done that you think is so bad?

11. Not only have I received the gift of second chances, I've had many opportunities to offer that gift as well. Being forgiven is important—but so is forgiving.

* Do you give up on people?
* Who's that one person you "kicked to the curb?" Why?
* What would go through your mind if you were in their shoes?
* Do you need to reach out to them?
* What's one step can you take today to forgive them and really mean it?

12. I start each morning thanking God for all the many blessings in my life. When I start my day being God-centered instead of Jon-centered, my day usually goes well. And having an attitude of gratitude places me in a positive mindset.

* How do you start your day?
* What is your first thought when you wake up?
* Do you take time to "get yourself going" in the morning?

*   If so, what do you do? If not, why?
*   Throughout the day, do you go on a "praise hunt" or would it be better described as a "sin hunt"?
*   Do you more naturally look for the good or the bad?
*   In what ways could you begin to change your mindset to be more positive?
*   What ten things are you grateful for?

13. One of the reasons I journal is to jog my memory of past events. I go back periodically and re-read what I wrote. Specifically, I look to see who I have been praying for. It always makes my heart smile when a prayer has been answered.

*   Do you journal?
*   If so, what do you write down?
*   How does journaling make you feel?
*   Do you go back and re-read what you have written?
*   Does anything stand out to you? If so, what?
*   Do you share your writing with anyone?
*   If you don't journal, what other tools do you use to remember the past?

14. I spent the majority of my life living on self-will. I thought I was weak if I could not do something myself and if I did not know all the answers. Subsequently, I was embarrassed to ask for help. And by not asking, no one knew I needed help. But when I finally reached out, I realized people *want* to help.

*   Do you have trouble asking for help?
*   What is it inside you that refuses to ask?
*   Think of a time when you could not do something on your own and you had no other options than to ask for help. Who did you ask?
*   How did they react?

* What did you need help doing?
* When they helped, how did you feel?
* Was it a good experience? Bad?
* What lessons did you learn?

15. I allowed fear to run my life for so long. I was scared of failing, scared of being fat, scared of not fitting in, scared of not being liked, scared of being alone. Fear has the potential to paralyze me if I allow it to. Experience tells me when I am fearful that surrendering my fears to God and taking the next step forward reduces or eliminates the fear. Things that I project to happen very seldom come true.

   * Describe your three biggest fears.
   * When have you experienced them?
   * How do they affect you?
   * What do you do to overcome them?
   * Have any of your fears come true?
   * What actions would you take if you valued yourself more? If you trusted yourself more?

16. I am often good at giving people advice on how to fix their problems. However, I am not always the best at fixing my own. It seems when I am going through something, my mind goes blank at what the solution would be.

   * Are you the same way?
   * What is the best advice you have given someone?
   * What's the best advice you have given yourself?
   * What's the best advice someone has given you?
   * Who do you seek when you have a problem?
   * Do they always have the solution?
   * When they tell you what they would do, is it an "a-ha" moment for you?

17. As a society, we often searching for "quick fixes." We want to have things change immediately for what we think is the better. I am the same way. In a snap, I want to change the way I feel, the way I look, etc.

* Describe when you have sought out a "quick fix."
* What was it you wanted to change? Why?
* What was the outcome?
* Did you spend money?
* Where did you go to find the solution?
* Did it provide a permanent fix or was it temporary?
* How do you find lasting fulfillment versus temporary pleasure?

18. I tend to make things more complicated than they really are. I can analyze something to death to the point of having no clarity. A friend once told me that living is very simple and if I remembered each day to trust God, clean house, and help others, then I would experience an abundant life. When I do, I find that to be true.

* Describe a time when you have trusted God 100 percent. What happened?
* How did it turn out?
* Describe a time when you accepted your part for a misunderstanding or a mishap without pointing fingers at anyone else.
* How did it turn out?
* How did it make you feel?
* How did the other person react?
* Describe a time when you have helped someone. How did it feel to be selfless?

19. Many times my self-talk has been very negative toward myself. *I am not good enough. I can't do that.* Over time, I believed what I was telling myself.

* What self-limiting beliefs do you have?
* What do you tell yourself over and over?
* Have you started to believe it?
* Is it influenced by what others have said about you? A particular situation?
* How has your mind changed the way you act?
* Do you continue to talk negatively to yourself?
* What are two steps you can take to eliminate the negative self-talk?

20. In addition to the negative self-talk, I am often my own worst critic. I can analyze to death my actions to the point of hating myself. *Why did (or didn't) I say that? Why did (or didn't) I do that?* I have a tough time forgiving myself at times. But no matter what I have done in the past or what I do in the future, God loves me. He will never stop. God also forgives me. I find peace and comfort in his forgiveness and love.

* Think of a time when you "beat yourself up" for something you said or did.
* What was it that you did or said so wrong? Why was it wrong?
* Were others involved? What did they say? Do?
* Did you eventually forgive yourself or are you still holding on to it?
* How has it affected your life?
* What would it look like in your life if you truly accepted that God loves you?
* How would it change the way you act and what you believe?

21. I spent a lot of my life trying to fit other people's God into my box. It didn't work well. However, I knew there was a power greater than me, so I continued to seek. As I remained

open-minded, I finally discovered a personal relationship with the God who meets me as *I* am.

* If someone asked you who God is to you, what would you say?
* Who has influenced your concept of God? And in what ways?
* Why has it impacted you?
* Has your viewpoint of God changed over the years?
* If so, in what ways?

22. When I hit rock bottom in 2010, I was willing and ready to do anything to eliminate the pain. I finally surrendered doing things my way and on my terms. I said, "Okay, God. I sure hope you have my back here."

* What does surrender mean to you?
* What does it look like? Feel like?
* We all need to surrender something. What are you hanging onto that you need to get rid of?
* Why is it hard to let go?
* Think of a time when you have surrendered something? Describe that time.
* Has God ever let you down when you surrendered something to him? Describe one time when he has come through for you.

23. What are the three most important things you want people to remember you by?

* Based on your behavior today, are your actions congruent with your legacy desire?
* If not, what must you do to reverse that persona?

24. When I accepted who I really am and became okay with being vulnerable with people, I began to experience personal growth. It was like a ton of bricks had been removed

from my shoulders. People began opening up with me regarding their struggles. Our hearts began to connect. Life took on a new meaning.

* What does *vulnerability* mean to you?
* Describe a time when you were vulnerable.
* Who were you vulnerable with?
* How did it affect your relationship?
* How did you feel to not hide behind the façade?
* What was the result?
* Why are you not vulnerable?
* What are you trying to protect?

25. There have been many times when I gained valuable instruction from hearing someone's story.

* Who do you most connect with? Why?
* You have something that someone needs to hear. What's your story?
* Have you shared your experiences with others?
* If so, what have others said?
* How have you helped them? What can they relate to?
* If not, why? What's stopping you?

ACKNOWLEDGMENTS

Writing this book has been one of the most challenging feats of my life. There were many times when I could have ripped up the pages and called it quits. In fact, I wanted to on numerous occasions. But it was during those times when I was reminded of the words of support and encouragement from people who love and care for me.

Mom, thanks for believing in me when I didn't think anyone else did. Your daily notes of encouragement were just what I needed. And thank you for always talking about God. It finally sank in! Do you think you can make me some chicken fried steak and gravy now? Please?

Dad, we lost you way too early, but I smile every time I think about you. You and I were on the same page, weren't we? Thanks for loving me just the way I was. I always felt secure when I was with you. We'll play catch one day in the future!

Ronnie, you are an awesome big brother. Your willingness to be there for me at any and all times is very selfless. Knowing that you have my back without any judgment means so much to me. I'm blessed to have a brother like you. It's so true: blood runs thicker than water!

Kylie and Jake, I love being your father! Thank you for being awesome kids. You help me keep life in perspective. Keep dreaming big! And guess what? I love you!

A special thanks to Charlie and Carolyn Matejowsky for believing in me and encouraging me to get out of my comfort zone. The magic really happens when I believe in the unbelievable.

A grand slam of thanks to Scott Nethery for your encouragement and support, but more importantly, your friendship. God knew what he was doing that day at the Kolache Factory, didn't he? There are no coincidences, only God-winks! You have stuck right by my side through thick and thin, and I will never forget that. Let's keep makin' it happen!

My heartfelt gratitude goes to Gloria Ejimbe for encouraging me to share my experiences and for nudging me to continue moving forward in the search for my purpose. Your words were uplifting and exactly what I needed to keep plugging away.

My sincere appreciation goes to Brian Harrison for the encouraging words prior to having a word written down. Your message propelled me into action and inspired me to complete this book.

A big high-five of thanks to Lee Driggers. The confidence you had in me carried me many days. You took a chance on me and you never gave up. Your walk was exactly like your talk and I watched every step. I am grateful God put you in my life!

A gigantic hug of gratitude to Ginger Kolbaba. I could not have done this without you. From the first time we spoke on the phone, I knew you were a Godsend to get me over the hump. I can't wait to see what God has in store through "our" book. You are the best!

And last but not least, thank you, Kary Oberbrunner, for your generosity in sharing your knowledge and time so freely on how to write and publish a book. You have helped me make a dream come true.

My life is so rich because of the people in it. I used to say I was lucky, but today I say I am blessed. And I am grateful for that. It is about time I give back what was given to me. And after all, isn't it true that the more you give, the more you receive?

ABOUT THE AUTHOR

From the time Jon Peters was six years old he wanted to play baseball. That's pretty much all he did. And he got really good at it. His dream was to be the best pitcher in the world.

In 1989, he became the United States' record holder for the most consecutive wins (fifty-three) by a high school pitcher, a record that still stands today. His high school career ended with a record of fifty-four wins and one loss, along with three consecutive Class 4A State Baseball Championships.

Jon is the first high school baseball player to grace the cover of *Sports Illustrated*. He has also appeared on local and national media outlets such as CNN, *Good Morning America*, *The Today Show*, ESPN, *People, The Wall Street Journal*, *Houston Chronicle*, and *Dallas Morning News*.

Following high school, Jon attended Texas A&M University on a baseball scholarship. After enduring four arm surgeries and months of rehabilitation, he gave up his dream of pitching and became an undergraduate assistant coach at A&M. He assisted in directing the 1993 A&M team to the Southwest Conference Title and a berth in the College World Series. He has also coached at Blinn College and McMurry University.

Jon has a B.S. (Texas A&M) and M.A. (Sam Houston) in kinesiology.

Jon is now business development manager with an oil and gas firm in the Houston area. His relationship style of selling has enabled him to be at the top of the leader board. He also shares his story about succeeding in the "game of life" as a speaker and writer.

Connect with Jon at JonPeters.org.

NEXT STEPS

Did you enjoy reading this book? If so, I'd appreciate your help in getting the word out about it. Here's what you can do (and it really does make a difference).

1. Tell your friends! Or better yet, buy them a copy.
2. Write a review on Amazon, Barnes & Noble, Goodreads, or any of the book reviewer platforms. Even a line or two helps.
3. Write or post about it on social media.
4. Pray for impact to come through this book.
5. Do a book study with your friends or small group.
6. Invite me to come speak at your next men's retreat, youth retreat, church service, small group/book group, or other event. (See the next page for more details.)
7. Like my Facebook page: www.facebook.com/jonpeters.org.

Thank you for your help. Remember when your dream fades, God's dream for you never does! Believe in the unbelievable!

BRING JON TO YOUR NEXT EVENT

Jon Peters is available for speaking engagements and would love to talk with you about how he can help make your next event a great one.

For more information on Jon's topics, schedule, or how he can customize a message specifically for your group, contact him at www.jonpeters.org.

CPSIA information can be obtained
at www.ICGtesting.com
Printed in the USA
LVOW13s1617120418
573255LV00011B/886/P